Professional Resumes Series

MW01205575

RESUMES
FOR
ADVERTISING
CAREERS

The Editors of
VGM Career Horizons

VGM Career Horizons
a division of *NTC Publishing Group*
Lincolnwood, Illinois USA

Library of Congress Cataloging-in-Publication Data

Resumes for advertising careers/the editors of VGM Career Horizons.

   p. cm.—(VGM professional resumes series)
ISBN 0-8442-4152-0
   1. Résumés (Employment) 2. Advertising—Vocational guidance.
I. VGM Career Horizons (Firm) II. Series: VGM's professional
resumes series.
HF5383.R43 1992
808'.06665-dc20

                                         92-24298
                                           CIP

Published by VGM Career Horizons, a division of NTC Publishing Group.
© 1993 by NTC Publishing Group, 4255 West Touhy Avenue,
Lincolnwood (Chicago), Illinois 60646-1975 U.S.A.

2 3 4 5 6 7 8 9 VP 9 8 7 6 5 4 3 2 1

ACKNOWLEDGMENT

The editors gratefully acknowledge Jeffrey S. Johnson and Cheryl McLean for their help in writing and production of this book.

CONTENTS

INTRODUCTION

Your resume is your first impression on a prospective employer. Though you may be articulate, intelligent, and charming in person, a poor resume may prevent you from ever having the opportunity to demonstrate your interpersonal skills, because a poor resume may prevent you from ever being called for an interview. While few people have ever been hired solely on the basis of their resume, a well-written, well-organized resume can go a long way toward helping you land an interview. Your resume's main purpose is to get you that interview. The rest is up to you and the employer. If you both feel that you are right for the job and the job is right for you, chances are you will be hired.

A resume must catch the reader's attention yet still be easy to read and to the point. Resume styles have changed over the years. Today, brief and focused resumes are preferred. No longer do employers have the patience, or the time, to review two or three pages of solid type. A resume should be only one page long, if possible, and never more than two pages. Time is a precious commodity in today's business world and the resume that is concise and straightforward will usually be the one that gets noticed.

Let's not make the mistake, though, of assuming that writing a brief resume means that you can take less care in preparing it. A successful resume takes time and thought, and if you are willing to make the effort, the rewards are well worth it. Think of your resume as a sales tool with the product being you. You want to sell yourself to a prospective employer. This book is designed to help you prepare a resume that will help you further your career—to land that next job, or first job, or to return to the work force after years of absence. So, read on. Make the effort and reap the rewards that a strong resume can bring to your career. Let's get to it!

Chapter One

THE ELEMENTS OF A GOOD RESUME

A winning resume is made of the elements that employers are most interested in seeing when reviewing a job applicant. These basic elements are the ingredients of a successful resume and are essential to any resume. These elements become the actual sections of your resume. The following is a list of elements that may be used in a resume. Some are essential; some are optional. We will be discussing these in this chapter in order to give you a better understanding of each element's role in the makeup of your resume:

1. Heading
2. Objective
3. Work Experience
4. Education
5. Licenses and Certificates
6. Professional Memberships
7. Honors
8. Activities
9. Special Skills
10. References

The first step in preparing your resume is to gather together all the information about yourself and your past accomplishments.

Later you will refine this information, rewrite it in the most effective language, and organize it into the most attractive layout. First, let's take a look at each of these important elements individually.

Heading

The heading may seem to be a simple enough element in your resume, but be careful not to take it lightly. The heading should be placed at the top of your resume and should include your name, home address, and telephone numbers. If you can take calls at your current place of business, include your business number, since most employers will attempt to contact you during the business day. If this is not possible, or if you can afford it, purchase an answering machine that allows you to retrieve your messages while you are away from home. This way you can make sure you don't miss important phone calls. *Always* include your phone number on your resume. It is crucial that when prospective employers need to have immediate contact with you, they can.

Objective

When seeking a particular career path, it is important to list a job objective on your resume. This statement helps employers know the direction that you see yourself heading, so that they can determine whether your goals are in line with the position available. The objective is normally one sentence long and describes your employment goals clearly and concisely.

Below are a few examples of job objectives as they might appear on a resume:

Example #1
OBJECTIVE: To join a small- to medium-sized public accounting firm with a near-term goal of partnership admission.

Example #2
OBJECTIVE: To secure a position as a paralegal where I can utilize my education, my writing, and my interpersonal skills.

Example #3
OBJECTIVE: A professional sales position, leading to management in the food industry, where my administrative experience, communications skills, and initiative can be utilized to increase sales and improve customer relations.

As you can see, the job objective will vary depending on the type of person you are and the type of goals you have. It can be either specific or general, but it should always be to the point.

This element in some cases is not necessary, but usually it is a good idea to include your objective. It gives your possible future employer an idea of where you are coming from and where you want to go.

Work Experience

This element is arguably the most important of them all. It will provide the central focus of your resume, so it is necessary that this section be as complete as possible. Only by examining your work experience in depth can you get to the heart of your accomplishments and present them in a way that demonstrates the strength of your qualifications. Of course, someone just out of school will have less work experience than someone who has been working for a number of years, but the amount of information isn't the most important thing—rather, how it is presented and how it highlights you as a person and as a worker will be what counts.

As you work on this section of your resume, be aware of the need for accuracy. You'll want to include all necessary information about each of your jobs, including job title, dates, employer, city, state, responsibilities, special projects, and accomplishments. Be sure to only list company accomplishments for which you were directly responsible. If you haven't participated in any special projects, that's all right—this area may not be relevant to certain jobs.

A basic rule of resume writing, and an extremely important one is: *List all work experience in reverse chronological order*. In other words, always start with your most recent job and work your way backwards. This way your prospective employer sees your current (and usually most important) job before seeing your less important past jobs. Your most recent position should also be the one that includes the most information, as compared to your previous positions. If you are just out of school, show your summer employment and part-time work, though your education will most likely be more important than your work experience in this case.

The following worksheets will help you gather information about your past jobs. Begin with your most recent job and work backwards.

WORK EXPERIENCE
Job One:

Job Title _____

Dates _____

Employer _____

City, State _____

Major Duties _____

_____

_____

_____

_____

_____

_____

_____

Special Projects _____

_____

_____

_____

Accomplishments _____

_____

_____

_____

_____

_____

_____

_____

_____

Job Two:

Job Title _____

Dates _____

Employer _____

City, State _____

Major Duties _____

_____

_____

_____

_____

_____

_____

_____

Special Projects _____

_____

_____

_____

Accomplishments _____

_____

_____

_____

_____

_____

_____

_____

_____

Job Three:

Job Title _____

Dates _____

Employer _____

City, State _____

Major Duties _____

_____

_____

_____

_____

_____

_____

_____

Special Projects _____

_____

_____

_____

Accomplishments _____

_____

_____

_____

_____

_____

_____

_____

Job Four:

Job Title _____

Dates _____

Employer _____

City, State _____

Major Duties _____

_____

_____

_____

_____

_____

_____

_____

Special Projects _____

_____

_____

_____

Accomplishments _____

_____

_____

_____

_____

_____

_____

_____

_____

Education

Education is the second most important element of a resume. Your educational background is often a deciding factor in an employer's decision to hire you. Be sure to stress your accomplishments in school with the same finesse that you stressed your accomplishments at work. If you are looking for your first job, your education will be your greatest asset, since your work experience will most likely be minimal. In this case, the education section becomes the most important. You will want to be sure to include any degrees or certificates you received, your major area of concentration, any honors, and any relevant activities. Again, be sure to list your most recent schooling first.

The following worksheets will help you gather information for this section of your resume. Also included are supplemental worksheets for honors and for activities. Sometimes honors and activities are listed in a section separate from education, most often near the end of the resume.

EDUCATION

School _____

Major or Area of Concentration _____

Degree _____

Date _____

School _____

Major or Area of Concentration _____

Degree _____

Date _____

School _____

Major or Area of Concentration _____

Degree _____

Date _____

Honors

Here, you should list any awards, honors, or memberships in honorary societies that you have received. Usually these are of an academic nature, but they can also be for special achievement in sports, clubs, or other school activities. Always be sure to include the name of the organization honoring you and the date(s) received, e.g., Dean's List, 1989, 1990. Use the worksheet below to help gather your honors information.

HONORS

Honor: _____

Awarding Organization: _____

Date(s): _____

Honor: _____

Awarding Organization: _____

Date(s): _____

Honor: _____

Awarding Organization: _____

Date(s): _____

Honor: _____

Awarding Organization: _____

Date(s): _____

Activities

You may have been active in different organizations or clubs during your years at school; often an employer will look at such involvement as evidence of initiative and dedication. Your ability to take an active role, and even a leadership role, in a group should be included on your resume. Use the worksheet provided to list your activities and accomplishments in this area.

ACTIVITIES

Organization/Activity: _____

Accomplishments: _____

_____

_____

Organization/Activity: _____

Accomplishments: _____

_____

_____

Organization/Activity: _____

Accomplishments: _____

_____

_____

Organization/Activity: _____

Accomplishments: _____

_____

_____

As your work experience increases through the years, your school activities and honors will play less of a role in your resume, and eventually you will most likely only list your degree and any major honors you received. This is due to the fact that, as time goes by, your job performance becomes the most important element in your resume. So, through time your resume should change to reflect this.

Certificates and Licenses

The next potential element of your resume is certificates and licenses. You should list these if the job you are seeking requires them and you, of course, have acquired them. If you have applied for a license, but have not yet received it, use the phrase "application pending."

License requirements vary by state. If you have moved or you are planning to move to another state, be sure to check with the appropriate board or licensing agency in the state in which you are applying for work to be sure that you are aware of all the necessary requirements.

Always be sure that all of the information you list is completely accurate. Locate copies of your licenses and certificates and check the exact date and name of the accrediting agency, e.g., Teaching Certificate, State of Illinois Board of Education, 1988. Use the following worksheet to list your licenses and certificates.

CERTIFICATES AND LICENSES

Name of License: _____

Licensing Agency: _____

Date Issued: _____

Name of License: _____

Licensing Agency: _____

Date Issued: _____

Name of License: _____

Licensing Agency: _____

Date Issued: _____

Professional Memberships

Another potential element in your resume is a section that lists professional memberships. Use this section to list any involvement in professional associations, unions, and similar organizations. It is to your advantage to list any professional memberships that pertain to the job you are seeking. Be sure to include the dates of your involvement and whether you took part in any special activities or held any offices within the organization, e.g., Society of Civil Engineers, 1986–present. Use the following worksheet to gather your information.

PROFESSIONAL MEMBERSHIPS

Name of Organization: _____

Offices Held: _____

Activities: _____

Date(s): _____

Name of Organization: _____

Offices Held: _____

Activities: _____

Date(s): _____

Name of Organization: _____

Offices Held: _____

Activities: _____

Date(s): _____

Name of Organization: _____

Offices Held: _____

Activities: _____

Date(s): _____

Special Skills

This section of your resume is set aside for mentioning any special abilities you have that could relate to the job you are seeking. Today, many employers seek applicants who have experience with computers. Be sure to list all types of computer hardware and software with which you have familiarity. Often, knowledge of a particular type of software is essential if the company you are interviewing with uses it exclusively. This is the part of your resume where you have the opportunity to demonstrate certain talents and experiences that are not necessarily a part of your educational or work experience.

Another beneficial special skill is knowledge of a foreign language. Just open a newspaper to the classified section, and you will notice the numerous job openings for those with bilingual skills. Be sure to mention if you are fluent or simply have a working knowledge of a foreign language. This will make a difference to your employer.

Special skills can encompass a wide range of your talents—from being a freelance editor to being an expert pilot. Remember to be sure that whatever skills you list relate directly or indirectly to the type of work you are looking for.

References

References are not usually listed on the resume, but a prospective employer needs to know that you have references who may be contacted if necessary. All that is necessary to include in your resume regarding references is a sentence at the bottom stating, "References are available upon request." This will suffice. A prospective employer may indeed wish to have a list of references, so be sure to have your list ready before you send out your resume. Also, check with whomever you list to see if it is all right for you to use them as a reference. Forewarn them that they may receive a call regarding a reference for you. This way they can be prepared to give you the best reference possible.

Chapter Two

WRITING YOUR RESUME

Now that you have gathered together all of the information for each of the sections of your resume, it's time to write out each section in a way that will get the attention of whoever is reviewing it. The type of language you use in your resume has a profound effect on its success. You want to take the information you have gathered and translate it into a language that will cause a potential employer to sit up and take notice.

Resume writing is not like expository writing or creative writing. It embodies a functional, direct writing style and focuses on the use of action words. By using action words in your writing, you more effectively stress past accomplishments. Action words help demonstrate your initiative and highlight your talents. Always use verbs that show strength and reflect the qualities of a "doer." For example, instead of "Put together a sales plan for the Midwest," use "Orchestrated a regional sales plan that increased sales in several midwestern states." Instead of "The newspaper was redesigned while I was managing editor," say "Served as managing editor. Redesigned newspaper's layout." By using action words, you characterize yourself as a person who takes action, and this will impress potential employers.

The following is a list of verbs commonly used in resume writing. Note that it is resume style to use the past tense (*-ed*) rather that the present. Use this list to choose the action words that can help your resume become a strong one:

administered

advised

analyzed

arranged

assembled

assumed responsibility

billed

built

carried out

channeled

collected

communicated

compiled

completed

conducted

contacted

contracted

coordinated

counseled

created

cut

designed

determined

developed

directed

dispatched

distributed

documented

edited

established

expanded

functioned as

gathered

handled

hired

implemented

improved

inspected

interviewed

introduced

invented

maintained

managed

met with

motivated

negotiated

operated

orchestrated

ordered

organized

oversaw

performed

planned

prepared

presented

produced

programmed

published

purchased

recommended

recorded

reduced

referred

represented

researched

reviewed

saved

screened

served as

served on

sold

suggested

supervised

taught

tested

trained

typed

wrote

Now let's take a look at the information you put down on the work experience worksheets. Take that information and rewrite it in paragraph form, using verbs to highlight your actions and accomplishments. Let's look at an example:

WORK EXPERIENCE

Job Title: Regional Sales Manager

Dates: 1988–1992

Employer: Pillsbury & Co.

City, State: Levittown, PA

Major Duties: Manager of sales representatives from seven states. Responsible for twelve food chain accounts in the east. In charge of directing the sales force in planned selling toward specific goals. Supervisor and trainer of new sales representatives. Consulting for customers in the areas of inventory management and quality control.

Special Projects: Coordinator and sponsor of annual food industry sales seminar.

Accomplishments: Monthly regional volume went up 25 percent during my tenure while, at the same time, a proper sales/cost ratio was maintained. Customer/company relations improved significantly.

Below is the rewritten version of this information, using action words. Notice how much stronger it sounds.

WORK EXPERIENCE

Pillsbury & Co., Levittown, PA

Regional Sales Manager, 1988–1992

Managed sales representatives from seven states. Handled twelve food chain accounts in the eastern United States. Directed the sales force in planned selling towards specific goals. Supervised and trained new sales representatives. Consulted for customers in the areas of inventory management and quality control. Coordinated and sponsored the annual Food Industry Seminar. Increased monthly regional volume 25 percent and helped to improve customer/company relations during my tenure.

This is the kind of direct, strong language necessary for a successful resume. Another way of constructing the work experience section is by using actual job descriptions. Job descriptions are rarely written using the proper resume language, but they do include all the information necessary to create this section of your resume. Take the description of one of the jobs you are including on your resume (if you have access to it), and turn it into an action-oriented paragraph. Below is an example of a job description followed by a version of the same description written using action words.

PUBLIC ADMINISTRATOR I

Responsibilities: Coordinate and direct public services to meet the needs of the nation, state, or community. Analyze problems; work with special committees and public agencies; recommend solutions to governing bodies.

Aptitudes and Skills: Ability to relate to and communicate with people; solve complex problems through analysis; plan, organize, and implement policies and programs. Knowledge of political systems; financial management; personnel administration; program evaluation; organizational theory.

WORK EXPERIENCE
State of California, Los Angeles, California

Public Administrator I, 1985–1990

Wrote pamphlets and conducted discussion groups to inform citizens of legislative processes and consumer issues. Organized and supervised crew of interviewers. Trained interviewers in effective communication skills.

Now that you have learned how to word your resume, you are ready for the next step in your quest for a winning resume: assembly and layout.

Chapter Three

ASSEMBLY AND LAYOUT

*A*t this point, you've gathered all the necessary information for your resume, and you've rewritten it using the language necessary to impress potential employers. Your next step is to assemble these elements in a logical order and then to lay them out on the page neatly and attractively in order to achieve the desired effect: getting that interview.

Assembly

The order of the elements in a resume makes a difference in its overall effect. Obviously, you would not want to put your name and address in the middle of the resume or your special skills section at the top. You want to put the elements in an order that stresses your most important achievements, not the less pertinent information. For example, if you recently graduated from school and have no full-time work experience, you will want to list your education before you list any part-time jobs you may have held during school. On the other hand, if you have been gainfully employed for several years and currently hold an important position in your company, you will want to list your work experience ahead of your education, which has become less pertinent with time.

There are some elements that are always included in your resume and some that are optional. On page 20 is a list of essential and optional elements:

Essential	*Optional*
Name	Job Objective
Address	Honors
Phone Number	Special Skills
Work Experience	Professional Memberships
Education	Activities
References Phrase	Certificates and Licenses

Your choice of optional sections depends on your own background and employment needs. Always use information that will put you and your abilities in a favorable light. If your honors are impressive, then be sure to include them in your resume. If your activities in school demonstrate particular talents necessary for the job you are seeking, then allow space for a section on activities. Each resume is unique, just as each person is unique.

Types of Resumes

So far, our discussion about resumes has involved the most common type—the *chronological resume*. In a chronological resume, all work experience is listed in reverse chronological order, with your most recent job first and so on. This is the type of resume usually preferred by human resources directors, and it is the one most frequently used. However, in some cases this style of presentation is not the most effective way to highlight your skills and accomplishments.

For someone reentering the work force after many years or someone looking to change career fields, the *functional resume* may work best. This type of resume focuses more on achievement and less on the sequence of your work history. In the functional resume, your experience is presented by what you have accomplished and the skills you have developed in your past work.

A functional resume can be assembled from the same information you collected for your chronological resume. The main difference lies in the use you make of this information. Essentially, the work experience section becomes two sections, with your job duties and accomplishments comprising one section and your employer's name, city, state, your position, and the dates employed making up another section. The first section is placed near the top of the resume, just below the job objective section, and can be called *Accomplishments* or *Achievements*. The second section, containing the bare essentials of your employment history, should come after the accomplishments section and can be titled *Work Experience* or *Employment History*. The other sections of your resume remain the same. The work experience section is the only one affected in the functional resume. By placing the section that focuses on your achievements first, you thereby draw attention to these achievements. This puts less emphasis on who you worked for and more emphasis on what you did and what you are capable of doing.

For someone changing careers, emphasis on skills and achievements is essential. The identities of previous employers, which may be unrelated to one's new job field, need to be downplayed. The functional resume accomplishes this task. For someone reentering the work force after many years, a functional resume is the obvious choice. If you lack full-time work experience, you will need to draw attention away from this fact and instead focus on your skills and abilities gained possibly through volunteer activities or part-time work. Education may also play a more important role in this resume.

Which type of resume is right for you will depend on your own personal circumstances. It may be helpful to create a chronological *and* a functional resume and then compare the two to find out which is more suitable. The sample resumes found in this book include both chronological and functional resumes. Use these resumes as guides to help you decide on the content and appearance of your own resume. One example each of chronological and functional resumes follows on the next two pages.

Layout

Once you have decided which elements to include in your resume and you have arranged them in an order that makes sense and emphasizes your achievements and abilities, then it is time to work on the physical layout of your resume.

There is no single appropriate layout that applies to every resume, but there are a few basic rules to follow in putting your resume on paper:

1. Leave a comfortable margin on the sides, top, and bottom of the page (usually 1 to 1½ inches).

2. Use appropriate spacing between the sections (usually 2 to 3 line spaces are adequate).

3. Be consistent in the *type* of headings you use for the different sections of your resume. For example, if you capitalize the heading EMPLOYMENT HISTORY, don't use initial capitals and underlining for a heading of equal importance, such as Education.

4. Always try to fit your resume onto one page. If you are having trouble fitting all your information onto one page, perhaps you are trying to say too much. Try to edit out any repetitive or unnecessary information or possibly shorten descriptions of earlier jobs. Maybe

CHRONOLOGICAL RESUME

DAVID P. JENKINS
3663 N. Coldwater Canyon
North Hollywood, CA 90390
818/555-3472
818/555-3678

JOB OBJECTIVE: A position as a sales/marketing manager where I can ultilize
my knowledge and experience by combining high volume selling
of major accounts with an administrative ability that increases
sales through encouragement of sales team.

EMPLOYMENT
HISTORY: Tribor Industries, Los Angeles, CA
Regional Sales Manager, 1985 - present
Managed sales of all product lines in western markets for a
leading maker of linens. Represented five corporate divisions
of the company with sales in excess of $3,000,000 annually.
Directed and motivated a sales force of 12 sales representatives
in planned selling to achieve company goals.

Tribor Industries, Los Angeles, CA
District Manager, 1980 - 1985
Acted as sales representive for the Los Angeles metropolitan
area. Built both wholesale and dealer distribution substantially
during my tenure. Promoted to Regional Sales Manager after five
years service.

American Office Supply, Chicago, IL
Assisant to Sales Manager, 1976 - 1980
Handled both internal and external areas of sales and marketing,
including samples, advertising and pricing. Served as company
sales representative and sold a variety of office supplies to
retail stores.

EDUCATION: University of Michigan, Ann Arbor, MI
B.A. Business Administration, 1975
Major Field: Management

SEMINARS: National Management Association Seminar, 1984
Purdue University Seminars, 1987, 1988

PROFESSIONAL
MEMBERSHIPS: Sales and Marketing Association of Los Angeles
National Association of Market Developers

REFERENCES: Available upon request

FUNCTIONAL RESUME

SARA WOODS
4400 Sunset Blvd.
Los Angeles, CA 90028
213/555-8989
213/555-6666

OBJECTIVE: A position in sales management.

ACHIEVEMENTS: * Planned successful strategies to identify and develop new accounts.
               * Increased sales by at least 20% each year as District Sales
                 Manager.
               * Researched and analyzed market conditions in order to seek out
                 new customers.
               * Developed weekly and monthly sales strategies.
               * Supervised seven sales representatives.
               * Conducted field visits to solve customer complaints.
               * Maintained daily customer contact to insure good customer/
                 company relations.
               * Wrote product information fliers and distributed them through
                 a direct mail program.

WORK
EXPERIENCE: <u>Southern California Fruit Co.</u>, Los Angeles, CA
               District Sales Manager, 1986 – present

               <u>L.A. Freight Co.</u>, Los Angeles, CA
               Account Executive, 1984 – 1986

               <u>Handlemen & Associates</u>, Santa Rita, CA
               Sales Representative, 1983 – 1984

EDUCATION: <u>University of Colorado</u>, Boulder, CO
               B.A., 1983
               Major: Management
               Minor: Political Science
               G.P.A. 3.3/4.0

PROFESSIONAL
MEMBERSHIPS: Southern California Sales Association, Treasurer, 1988 – 1990
               Los Angeles Chamber of Commerce, 1986 – present

SPECIAL
SKILLS: DOS experience. LOTUS/DBASE/WORD PERFECT experience.

REFERENCES: Provided on request

you've included too many optional sections. Don't let the idea of having to tell every detail about your life get in the way of producing a resume that is simple and straightforward. The more compact your resume, the easier it will be to read and the better impression it will make for you.

Try experimenting with various layouts until you find one that looks good to you. It may be a good idea to show your final layout to people who can tell you what they think is right or wrong with it. Ask them what impresses them most about your resume. Make sure that is what you want most to emphasize. If it isn't, you may want to consider making changes in your layout until the necessary information is emphasized. Use the sample resumes in chapter 5 to get some ideas for laying out your resume.

Putting Your Resume in Print

Your resume should be typed or printed on good quality 8½″ × 11″ bond paper. You want to make as good an impression as possible with your resume; therefore, quality paper is a necessity. If you have access to a word processor with a good printer, make use of it. If not, a typewriter that produces good, clean copy should be just fine.

After you have produced a clean original, you will want to go ahead and make duplicate copies of it. Usually a copy shop is your best bet for producing copies without smudges or streaks. Make sure you have the copy shop use quality bond paper for all copies of your resume. Ask for a sample copy before they run your entire order. After copies are made, check each copy for cleanliness and clarity.

Another more costly option is to have your resume typeset and printed by a printer. This will provide the most attractive resume, but most likely the neat, clean, hand-typed resume will have the same effect as the typeset resume at far less expense.

Proofreading

After you have finished typing the master copy of your resume and before you go to have it copied or printed, you must thoroughly check it for typing and spelling errors. Have several people read it over just in case you may have missed an error. Misspelled words and typing mistakes will not make a good impression on a prospective employer. They are a bad reflection on your writing ability and your attention to detail. With thorough and conscientious proofreading, these mistakes can be avoided. The following are some rules of capitalization and punctuation that may come in handy when proofreading your resume:

Rules of Capitalization

- Capitalize proper nouns, such as names of schools, colleges and universities, names of companies, and brand names of products.
- Capitalize major words in the names and titles of books, tests, and articles that appear in the body of your resume.
- Capitalize words in major section headings of your resume.
- Do not capitalize words just because they seem important.
- When in doubt, consult a manual of style such as *Words Into Type* (Prentice-Hall); or *The Chicago Manual of Style*, (The University of Chicago Press). Your local library can help you locate these and others.

Rules of Punctuation

- Use a comma to separate words in a series.
- Use a semicolon to separate series of words that already include commas within the series.
- Use a semicolon to separate independent clauses that are not joined by a conjunction.
- Use a period to end a sentence.
- Use a colon to show that the examples or details that follow expand or amplify the preceding phrase.
- Avoid the use of dashes.
- Avoid the use of brackets.
- If you use any punctuation in an unusual way in your resume, be consistent in its use.
- Whenever you are uncertain, consult a style manual.

Chapter Four

THE COVER LETTER

*O*nce your resume has been assembled, laid out, and printed to your satisfaction, the next and final step before distribution is to write your cover letter. Though there may be instances where you deliver your resume in person, most often you will be sending it through the mail. Resumes sent through the mail always need an accompanying letter that briefly introduces you and your resume. The purpose of the cover letter is to get a potential employer to read your resume, just as the purpose of your resume is to get that same potential employer to call you for an interview.

Like your resume, your cover letter should be clean, neat, and direct. A cover letter usually includes the following information:

1. Your name and address (unless it already appears on your personal letterhead).

2. The date.

3. The name and address of the person and company to whom you are sending your resume.

4. The salutation ("Dear Mr." or "Dear Ms." followed by the person's last name, or "To Whom It May Concern" if you are answering a blind ad).

5. An opening paragraph explaining why you are writing (in response to an ad, the result of a previous meeting, at the suggestion of someone you both know) and indicating that you are interested in whatever job is being offered.

6. One or two more paragraphs that tell why you want to work for the company and what qualifications and experience you can bring to that company.

7. A final paragraph that closes the letter and requests that you be contacted for an interview.

8. The closing ("Sincerely," or "Yours Truly," followed by your signature with your name typed under it).

Your cover letter, including all of the information above, should be no more than one page in length. The language used should be polite, businesslike, and to the point. Do not attempt to tell your life story in the cover letter. A long and cluttered letter will only serve to put off the reader. Remember, you only need to mention a few of your accomplishments and skills in the cover letter. The rest of your information is in your resume. Each and every achievement does not need to be mentioned twice. If your cover letter is a success, your resume will be read and all pertinent information reviewed by your prospective employer.

Producing The Cover Letter

Cover letters should always be typed individually, since they are always written to particular individuals and companies. Never use a form letter for your cover letter. Cover letters cannot be copied or reproduced like resumes. Each one should be as personal as possible. Of course, once you have written and rewritten your first cover letter to the point where you are satisfied with it, you certainly can use similar wording in subsequent letters.

After you have typed your cover letter on quality bond paper, be sure to proofread it as thoroughly as you did your resume. Again, spelling errors are a sure sign of carelessness, and you don't want that to be a part of your first impression on a prospective employer. Make sure to handle the letter and resume carefully to avoid any smudges, and then mail both your cover letter and resume in an appropriate sized envelope. Be sure to keep an accurate record of all the resumes you send out and the results of each mailing.

Numerous sample cover letters appear at the end of the book. Use them as models for your own cover letter or to get an idea of how cover letters are put together. Remember, every one is unique and depends on the particular circumstances of the individual writing it.

Now your job is complete. You can let your cover letter and resume do the rest and land you that interview that very well could lead to the job you are seeking.

Chapter Five

SAMPLE RESUMES

This chapter contains dozens of sample resumes for people pursuing a wide variety of jobs and careers. There are many different styles of resumes in terms of graphic layout and presentation of information. These samples also represent people with varying amounts of education and work experience. Use these samples to model your own resume after. Choose one resume, or borrow elements from several different resumes to help you construct your own.

BRENDA STEVENSON
108 Tierra del Sol Avenue #205
Denver, Colorado 80205
303/555-2655

Objective

Advertising career with advancement opportunities

Education

Bachelor of Arts, Business Administration, December 1989.
Adams State College, Alamosa, Colorado. Emphasis in Advertising.

Experience

Clerk/Typist. 1986-89.
Adams State College, Extended Studies Office
Richardson Hall, Room 143, Alamosa, Colorado 81102.

Duties included word processing on AT&T computers, answering customer questions and telephone calls, training new employees, enrolling students by computer, and sending out bulk mailings.

Receptionist. Summer 1985.
Rio Grande Savings and Loan
2209 Main, Denver, Colorado 81101.

Duties included answering telephones, scheduling appointments, filing, and assisting customers.

Sales Clerk 1979-84.
Sears, Roebuck and Company
514 Main Street, Alamosa, Colorado 81101.

Duties included customer service, obtaining catalog orders, answering telephones, filing, checking in freight, and teletyping.

Activities

Member of the American Advertising Federation.
Active in Alamosa community softball and volleyball leagues.

References

Available on request

Tammy Blakewood
2500 Francisco Blvd.
Pacifica, CA 94044
415 555-7883

Summary of Qualifications

More than 10 years experience in positions demanding organizational, administrative, and interpersonal skills. Adept at handling situations requiring prompt, tactful decisions. Highly motivated and dependable. Work well with people at all levels.

Experience

Blakewood & Associates, 24160 N. Beach Dr., Pacifica, CA 94045
<u>Owner/Sole-Proprietorship</u>
February 1988-October 1991

Structured and created desktop publishing and advertising services enterprise, based in a town of approximately 10,000. Primary activities included basic graphic design and laser typesetting for a quick print shop. Designed and created camera ready art for a tabloid for the Combined Counties Police Association that consisted of a 24-page, two-color display section and a 20-page editorial section with electronically scanned halftones. Sold the business turn-key, including all equipment and 20 hours of training and consulting.

H.H.S. and B. Advertising, 55 Oviedo Court, Pacifica, CA 94044.
<u>Operations Manager</u>
March 1979-February 1987
Originally hired as an entry level advertising account representative for a small agency. Assumed responsibility for all client reconciliations and billing, personnel scheduling, training and management, print media planning and placement, and outside print production contracting. Gradually developed and maintained efficient office management forms and systems program. Produced print media for publication in *The San Francisco Chronicle, The Oakland Tribune,* and *The Wall Street Journal* using desktop publishing. Gained industry experience in radio and television concept, copywriting, and production. Acquired practical experience in writing press releases and establishing and maintaining media contacts. Supervised the gathering, compilation, calculation and final presentation of demographic and psychographic data for use in marketing and advertising strategies. At all times personally assumed bottom line responsibility for deadlines and client satisfaction.

Dusk Magazine, Fremont, CA 94538
Owner/Sole-Proprietorship
January 1971- November 1979
Published monthly regional entertainment guide. Employed and supervised a sales manager and a distribution person.

Special Skills

Macintosh and IBM with various software including PageMaker, Works, Excel, Lotus 1-2-3, Tapscan Media Reach, Fast-Pak Mail, and The Editor.

Education

A.A. in Design, 1988; A.A. in Advertising, 1970
Pacifica College, Pacifica, CA

References available on request

JANE BREEN
3804 N DAMEN #1
MILWAUKEE, WI 53201
414 / 555-5616

EMPLOYMENT

1989-present – MAGNAN & ASSOCIATES ADVERTISING
345 North Canal, Suite 1402, Milwaukee, WI
Executive Director
Art direction, design, layout, computer graphics, freelance management, and copywriting. Obtain sources for vendors and suppliers. Implement computer graphics systems.
Clients: Schwinn Biclycle Corp.; Rand McNally, TDM; Sassy (baby products); Guarantee Trust Life Insurance; Margie's Bridal.

1989-present— FREELANCE (Milwaukee)
Clients: Beltone (BEC Advertising); Davidson Marketing Services Inc; MB Pasternak Associates; Wooster-Magnani Advertising; Roman, Inc.

1981-88 – BREEN GRAPHICS (Chicago)
Executive Director
Directed projects from initial client contact through camera-ready art. Concept and strategy development. Design, production, line and graphic illustration. Contracted for typesetters, camera work, printers, freelance photography, keyline, and illustration. Managed finances and billing.
Clients: WARM 98FM; Spectrum Publishing, Inc.; Forest View Gardens Restaurant; KELore International Nailcare; The Creative Factory; I.A. Associates; The Finishing Touch Interiors; Deltex Systems; The Downtowner Newspaper; Business Type Services; and The Under 5th Cafe.

1986-88 – ANTONELLI INSTITUTE OF ART
125 East 7th Street, Cincinnati, OH
Commercial Art Instructor/Advertising Coordinator
Taught Typography, Production Art I & II, Product Illustration, Layout, Graphic Design, Computer Graphics, Corporate Campaign Direction, and Drawing. Created and implemented curriculum changes to incorporate new computer graphics program.

1976-86 – WIII-TV 64
5177 Fishwick Drive, Cincinnati, OH
Art Director
Design and production of all print and outdoor advertising. TV Guide and local newspaper ads, billboards and busboards, sales and promotional materials including brochures, contest materials, posters, letterheads, camera cards, storyboards and sign painting; news and ID photography. Obtained vendor sources. Worked closely with marketing manager in selecting appropriate advertising vehicles.

1975-76 – PANAX PUBLISHING COMPANY, Lansing, MI
Paste-up Artist

EDUCATION

1981 B.F.A. Fine Arts, Indiana University (Graphic Design concentration)
Other Education: Computer Seminar Training, CBSD Teacher Training, Milwaukee Art Academy

REFERENCES

Available on request

KIMBERLY ANNE MORLEY
753 Elmore Drive
Little Rock, Arkansas 72202
501/555-1047

OBJECTIVE

Account executive position with small, independent advertising firm.

EXPERIENCE

Arkansas Sun Times Corporation, Pioneer Press Publishing Company, Little Rock

Display Advertising Account Executive, 1988 - present
Service and develop $350,000 territory for 38 suburban weekly newspapers.
Technical knowledge of advertising, design, pre-press and printing functions.
Experience in budgeting, pricing strategies, and proposal writing.
Coordinate local advertising promotions.

Stone Container Corporation, Tempe, AZ

Marketing Coordinator, 1987 - 1988
Coordinated and produced marketing and promotional materials and activities for leading
  international packaging company.
Organized and produced special events.
Produced quarterly design awards program.
Participated in development and production of Stone sales literature.
Designed sales presentations using computer.

EDUCATION

Columbia College, Chicago, Illinois
Bachelor of Arts, Liberal Arts-January, 1987—with honors

Arizona State University, Tempe, Arizona
Associate in Arts, Graphics Arts Processes/Photography, 1985

REFERENCES: Available upon request.

JOSEPH D. CAROTHERS
98 EAST 150TH STREET
BLOOMINGTON, IN 42167
812 - 555-9509

OBJECTIVE   Traffic/Production Manager for advertising agency or corporate advertising division.

EXPERIENCE

* Management of creative efforts and staff operations in graphic arts, illustration and photography for the publishing and advertising industry.

* Design and layout direction for magazine covers and articles, packaging, TV storyboards, advertising, point-of-sale promotions, brochures, books, posters, direct mail, and displays.

* Supervised editorial layout, art work, typography, and production, working with senior-management in coordination of production operations and general business functions.

* Staff training and supervision; budget planning; work flow scheduling and administrative management.

* Direct client services and sales support; vendor evaluation and contract negotiation.

* Work closely with the sales and marketing staff of advertising agency.

* Supervise freelance illustrators, art directors, and designers on special projects.

* Initiate concepts for print advertising and marketing campaigns.

* Art and production department management; all levels of creative support and public relations.

EDUCATION

Colorado Institute of Art, BFA 1973
Advertising Design--Graduated 'Top Designer" out of 125

Texas Tech University, AA 1971
Commercial Art, Architectural Design & Construction

School of Modern Photography
Advertising Photography coursework, 1990-1991

Indiana Institute of Technology
Business Management coursework, 1987-1988

EMPLOYMENT HISTORY

1988-1991 Design Marc Advertising Inc., Bloomington, IN
Creative Art Director

1987-1988 Amway Corporation, Cincinnati, OH
Art Director-Supervisor of Publications and Advertising

1985-1987 Crain Communication, Chicago, IL
Art Director/Modern Healthcare Magazine

1974-1984 American Bar Association Press, Chicago, IL
Creative Art Director

REFERENCES AVAILABLE

MARGARET M. JANSEN
11 Parkside Lane, No. 265
Salt Lake City, Utah 84115
(801) 555-9863

EDUCATION

University of Utah
Salt Lake City, Utah
Master of Science in Marketing, 1985

Patterson State College
Ogden, Utah
Bachelor of Science in Business, 1968

EMPLOYMENT HISTORY

Marketing/Advertising Director, Guardian State Bank, 1991-present
    Research target markets and competitive markets.
    Prepare complete marketing plan for introduction of new banking services.
    Design artwork and coordinate production.
    Design and prepare in-house art and informational materials.

Advertising Coordinator, Utah Waterline, 1985-1990
    Prepared advertising artwork and copy.
    Sold advertising space.

Accountant, Dickinson & Associates, 1976-1982
    Collected data and prepared weekly, monthly, and yearly reports.
    Prepared cost and profit reports, generated revision reports.
    Communicated with banks and other financial institutions.

Computer Support Specialist, Megawest, Inc., 1968-1976
    Provided instruction for clients in the use of accounting software.
    Provided basic accounting instruction and training in the preparation of income statements and
        balance sheets.
    Prepared reports with line specifications and custom features.
    Provided additional support for all software users.

REFERENCES

    Available as requested

CAMMY WINTERS • 5249 SW 9TH AVENUE • SEATTLE, WA 98006 • 206/555-2332

OBJECTIVE

A challenging position in advertising graphic design.

SKILLS

Extensive experience with typography, layout, paste-up, production and printing.
Ability to thoroughly research, organize, and manage projects from concept to completion.
Ability to communicate effectively with clients, in verbal and written form.
Solid working knowledge of Macintosh desktop publishing and graphics software
applications.

EDUCATION AND TRAINING

Washington State University
Bachelor of Fine Arts, Printmaking, 1987

University of Washington
Communications, 1983-84

PROFESSIONAL EXPERIENCE

Union Square Gazette, Seattle, WA
October 1989-present

Ad Production Clerk, II
All aspects of ad production, including dispatching of ads into system for production, input
into computer system for typesetting, layout and past-up, cutting color, proofreading,
running proofs, taking corrections over the phone or counter, delivery of ads as requested by
advertiser and layout and paste-up of the classified section. Required constant communication
with co-workers in the sales and production departments, clear communication with clients
and the ability to meet deadlines.

Old Town Desktop Publishing, Olympia, WA
February 1988-October 1989

Art Director/Production Manager
Design and production, including typesetting, page layout, paste-up, illustration, and liaison
with color house and printer.

Graphic Designer
Design, layout, and production for client specific projects. Experience with PageMaker,
FreeHand, WORD, MacDraw, VersaScan, Illustrator, Persuasion, and Cricket Graph.

References and portfolio furnished on request

Sam L. Chen

1362 W. 11th
Amherst, MA 01002
(413) 555-3889

Objective

Production Department Management in a progressive advertising firm.

Skills and Attributes

Publication

Familiar with entire publication process, from initial drafts to final distribution. Direct experience with planning, writing, editing, design, layout and production of various documents and publications.

Computers/Desktop Publishing

Experienced with Macintosh-based desktop publishing systems, including graphic design and page layout software and photo-imagesetting techniques. Familiar with wide range of software on both Macintosh and MS-DOS personal computer systems; exposure to and use of UNIX-based systems.

Interpersonal Skills

Able to relate extremely well with others, including situations which involve diverse groups of people or stressful interactions. Experience and training in empathic listening, assertiveness, cultural awareness, interviewing, teaching, and group/interpersonal processes.

Employment

Editor/Director, October 1988-present
Computer Engineering Network, College of Engineering
University of Massachusetts, Amherst, MA 01002

Write, layout and assist in all aspects of producing the CEN Newsletter, an award-winning, 16-page, monthly newsletter. Write and edit technical and feature articles for the newsletter. Layout and design of various other publications, including brochures, technical documentation, and handbooks. Coordinate and schedule production.

Executive Director/Administrative Assistant, February 1985 through October 1987
Neighborhood Housing Services, Easthampton, MA

Assessment and intake of clients for housing rehabilitation and purchase programs designed for low and moderate income persons. Managed revolving loan fund, including loan and credit counseling and servicing for high-risk loan profile. Created and designed homesteading program; obtained grants, contracts and coordinated fundraising for administration of all programs. Supervised construction and rehabilitation projects, public relations, and community organization efforts.

Assistant Manager/Sales Associate, December 1977 through February 1985
Smith Brothers Limited, Amherst, MA

Sales, customer relations, buying and ordering.

Education

University of Massachusetts, Amherst, MA. Bachelor of Arts, 1976.
Honors Program, College of Literature, Science and the Arts. 3.66 G.P.A.

College courses at other institutions: computer applications, real estate, property management.
Fifteen credits, 4.0 G.P.A.

Workshops and seminars on computer applications and systems, marketing, graphic design, fundraising, public relations, agency administration, finance, business law, and real estate.

Related Experience

Served as member of various boards and committees for the City of Easthampton from 1986-1988, including the Community Relations Board (Secretary) and the Pesticide-Herbicide Advisory Committee.

Volunteer service to SOS Community Crisis Center in Springfield, MA, from 1978-1981, including phone and walk-in crisis work, on-call crisis team member, on-going counselor, trainer, peer supervisor, and clinical program coordinator.

References Available Upon Request

MARY E. GLANCY
72 College Street
Beloit, Wisconsin 53511
(608) 555-4267

OBJECTIVE   To secure a position in advertising copywriting.

Beloit College, Beloit, Wisconsin
Bachelor of Arts in Journalism, August 1991
Minors in Creative Writing and Multicultural Studies

Honorable Mention, Thorpe Prize for Creative Writing, 1990.

Courses included: Journalism, Advertising Writing, Campaign Management and Strategic Planning, Advertising Account Management, Business Communications, and Creative Writing

COMPUTER SKILLS

On Macintosh, IBM-PC and Apple IIgs computers, have working knowledge of the following software: Quark XPress, MS Word, MacWrite, PageMaker, CricketGraph, FreeHand, Illustrator, Mousewrite, Multiscribe GS, Word Perfect, and Appleworks.

SUPPORTING EXPERIENCE

- Served as advertising coordinator for weekly college newspaper, 1989-90
- Attended Desktop Publishing Workshop for professional training in use of Quark XPress software program, April, 1989
- Worked as copyeditor for college newspaper, fall 1988
- Assisted as copyeditor for professor's philosophy dissertation, 1988
- Contributed as reporter and photographer for college paper, 1986-90
- Served as English tutor for Japanese college students, 1988-89
- Assisted in producing and circulating bi-monthly newsletter for Women's Center

ADDITIONAL EXPERIENCE

Also worked as substitute teacher, child care provider, preschool instructor, restaurant server, cook, and busperson, as newspaper deliverer, cashier, office aide, caterer, and ski chair lift operator.

COLLEGE ACTIVITIES

Active as varsity athlete in softball and soccer, volunteer with the admissions office, and as an Outing Club member. Member of Students for an Integrated Curriculum and Beloit College Women's Center.

REFERENCES AVAILABLE UPON REQUEST

Karl M. Landon
156 N. 25th Street • Arlington, Texas 75234 • 817 555-8678

Career Objective:

To create and manage professional, results-oriented advertising in a challenging environment.

Education:

Bachelor of Science, Journalism/Advertising
1983 Texas Wesleyan University

Skills and Achievements:

• Directed national advertising campaigns from concept development to media placement.

• Six years of progressively more responsible experience in managing the in-house advertising agency of an international corporation.

• Ability to handle every aspect involved in publishing a monthly magazine.

• Small staff supervisory experience.

• Bachelor of Science degree with a major in Journalism and a strong emphasis in Advertising.

• Computer fluent with IBM and Macintosh systems running word processing and desktop publishing software.

Experience:

Self Employed Creative Director, 1991-present.
Created an advertising and publications service. Responsible for new business development and managing existing account activity. Publish a monthly 20-page, high-quality magazine for one client. Provide writing, editing, proofing, photography, design, layout, production management, advertising sales, and mailing. Assist on production of a monthly business newspaper. Desktop publishing accounts for 40% of daily activities.

Director of Advertising, Border Burritos, Inc. 1984-1990.
Coordinated all national and regional advertising efforts for this 200-store fast food restaurant chain. Supervised all creative development and broadcast production through an outside agency. Developed all collateral print production. Supervised regional media buying for a 56-store co-op. Created all corporate self-promotion materials.

Media Buyer, January-November, 1984.
Television and radio buyer for the Texas Marketing Association, a 56-store media co-op.

Student Intern, June-December, 1983.
Media Buyer for company-owned restaurants in Arlington; research assistant on regionally conducted image and awareness survey; developed, produced, and implemented an in-store customer response survey; evaluated all company store sales results from advertising campaigns.

Newsletter Editor, Texas Ad Club, 1988-1990.
Writer, editor, and producer of the monthly "Ad Focus" published for the 500 members of the Texas Ad Club; other responsibilities included advertising sales and operation of the newsletter via the solicitation of sponsor donations of design time, paper and printing.

Other activities:
Board of Directors,Texas Ad Club
Individual Sponsor, American Advertising Museum
Speaker, 1990 Texas Wesleyan Journalism School Career Day
Award of Excellence and Achievement, Texas Ad Club

References available on request

Jolene E. Marks
3335 North Road
Bellevue, Colorado 80512
303 555-4886

job sought

A position in advertising sales with a daily newspaper.

education

Colorado State University, Fort Collins, CO: Bachelor of Arts in Journalism, news/editorial concentration, December, 1992.

Valley College, Rockland, PA: Completed three semesters of liberal arts courses, awarded High Honors on the Dean's honor list each semester, nominated to Phi Theta Cappa, academic fraternity. 1983-1984.

East High School, Rockland PA: Honors and activities included National Merit Scholar Recognition; National Honor Society member; Rockland Women's Club Poetry Contest winner; President, Girl's Madrigal Choir; Co-Captain and Most Valuable Player, Field Hockey team.

work history

Advertising Account Assistant: Bolling Publishing Co., May-August 1988. 25 Prospect Avenue, Redondo Beach, CA 90277. 213 555-8967. Internship sponsored by Business Educational Foundation. Developed advertising base accounts, prepared sales presentations, closed sales, assisted with billing and record keeping.

Advertising Sales: *Movement, Inc.* magazine, 1985-1988. 332 Linden Drive, Fort Collins, CO 80524. 303 555-3987. Duties included ad sales, ad copywriting, producing pages via desktop publishing, fulfilling circulation, and maintaining relations with advertisers and production department. Promoted from secretary to editor.

Other work experience: Nurses's Aide, Fall Lake Health Care; Receptionist, Rockland Animal Hospital; Lab Assistant, Valley College; Stable Hand, Treeline Stables; and Cashier, Rix Restaurant.

volunteer

Family Help Program, Rockland, PA. 1980-83. Worked one-on-one as a "big sister" to young girls who had been physically or sexually abused.

Crisisline, Rockland, PA. 1982-83. Graduated from 70-hour training program. Volunteered as line worker. Fielded phone calls ranging from information/referral to suicide prevention.

references

available on request

IAN P. ROBINSON
1009 Selby Drive, Geneva, Illinois 60134
Home (708) 555-9984 • Work (708) 555-0228

OBJECTIVE

Advertising account manager with responsibility for developing and implementing advertising campaigns. Especially interested in opportunities that will take advantage of my verbal and written fluency in French.

PROFESSIONAL EXPERIENCE

Genève Amerique, Geneva, IL. Manager and Buyer, 1988-current.
- Develop, produce and implement direct mail and newspaper advertising campaigns that have directly contributed to a 45% sales growth over four years.
- Buy and merchandise French textile and ceramic handcrafted items.
- Maintain financial control of $175,000 annual sales volume.
- Translate business-related documents French-English/English-French.

Storefront Bookstore, Minneapolis, MN. Manager / Regional Planner, 1987-1988.
- Responsible for effective visual presentation for three area stores.
- Trained and supervised ten employees.
- Controlled inventory and financial planning of $300,000 annual sales volume.

La France, Edina, MN. Counter Manager, 1984-1986.
- Supervised staff of twelve waiters.
- Supervised food preparation and distribution.
- Integrated daily cash receipts into restaurant financial budget.

KSMR Radio, Collegeville, MN. Assistant Director of Programming, 1985-1987. News Announcer/DJ, 1983-1985.
- Hired and scheduled staff of 75 volunteer disc jockeys.
- Implemented listener survey which increased funding by 63 percent.
- Wrote and engineered news programming and public service announcements.

EDUCATION

St. John's University, Collegeville, MN.
Bachelor of Arts in Government and French, awarded 1987.

Institute for American Universities, Aix-en-Provence, France.
French language coursework, 1986.

University of Chicago, Chicago, IL.
Specialized coursework in photography, 1989.
Specialized coursework in desktop publishing and design, 1990.

REFERENCES AVAILABLE

Richard Walker

ADDRESS	2774 Tower Drive, Chicago, IL 60647. (708) 555-8831
CAREER OBJECTIVE	To obtain a position that would both challenge and utilize my communication, desktop publishing, and graphic design talents.
EDUCATION	**Illinois State University** Bachelor of Science Degree, May 1988. **Major:** Visual and Written Communication. Grade Point Average: 4.0 (major)/3.5 (overall)

WORK EXPERIENCE

5/91 - present	**RW Graphics,** Chicago, IL. *Free Lance Desktop Publisher/Designer.* Involved in several free lance projects, including Production Editor and Art Director of The College News, a monthly independent publication; production of brochures and promotional packages for small businesses; and advertising creation, design, and production for small businesses.
10/90 - 5/91	**Week's Worth Magazine,** Lake Zurich, IL. *Editor and Designer.* Started weekly arts, culture, and entertainment magazine, gaining a circulation base of 14,000 within four months. Managed all aspects of marketing and promotion. Supervised advertising department staff for ad sales and self-promotion advertising campaigns. Managed all aspects of production. Assigned staff articles and edited free lance articles for publication. Designed magazine from cover to cover. Managed budget and payroll for 15-person staff.
4/90 - 12/90	**Friday's Magazine,** Daily Vidette, Illinois State University, Normal IL. *Editor.* Assigned and edited staff stories. Created page layout and design. Wrote feature-length stories. Managed budget and 8-person staff for weekly entertainment magazine supplement to college newspaper.
8/90 - 12/90	**College of Arts and Sciences,** Illinois State University, Normal, IL. *Newsletter Editor.* Created 8-page newsletter using Quark XPress. Interviewed faculty and student leaders. Wrote feature stories. Managed all aspects of production, including photography. Handled distribution network.
8/89 - 5/91	**Daily Vidette,** Illinois State University, Normal, IL. *Feature Writer and Columnist.* Covered various entertainment events, wrote feature stories and weekly commentary column for Features department.
1/90 - 5/90	**Department of Communication,** Illinois State University, Normal, IL. *Undergraduate Teaching Assistant.* Community Relations Department. Assisted students in the creation, design, layout, and writing of a newsletter produced in PageMaker on the Macintosh.
HONORS & AWARDS	Dean's List **General Assembly Scholar** **Critical Film Review Award,** Second Place, Illinois College Press Association **Graphic Illustration Award,** Second Place, Illinois College Press Association **Public Relations Student Society of America**
SPECIAL SKILLS	Thorough knowledge of desktop publishing and design programs, including Quark XPress and Aldus PageMaker. Also have desktop graphics and writing experience using IBM and Macintosh software applications.

REFERENCES AND PORTFOLIO AVAILABLE UPON REQUEST

JULIA D. MEIERSON
RFD 1 BOX 119
OAKLAND, MAINE 04963
(207) 555-1103

PRESENT EMPLOYMENT

The Square Cafe, Waterville, Maine   Since June, 1990
Primary responsibilities include designing and buying advertisements in local media, coordinating schedule of advertising, coordinating art gallery.

EDUCATION

Bates College, Lewiston, Maine   January 1983 to December 1986
Bachelor of Arts with High Honors in Anthropology and Religion
Honors Thesis: *Feminist Witchcraft: A Theological Analysis*

Activities:
Coordinator of Forum on Human Awareness, 1986
Coordinator of Womyn's Awareness, 1986
Dean's List

University of Jaffna, Jaffna, Sri Lanka   Fall semester, 1984
Conducted independent field study on maternity and child welfare.

University of Nottingham, Nottingham, England   Winter and Spring semesters, 1985
Conducted independent project at an abused women's shelter, working primarily with children of abused women.

The Evergreen State University, Olympia, Washington   Summer semester 1986
Studied ecological agriculture at TESC Organic Farm.

ADDITIONAL WORK EXPERIENCE

Rape Crisis Assistance, Inc., Waterville, Maine   January 1989 to May 1990
Co-director, coordinated volunteers and provided community education in Somerset County.

Family Planning, Skowhegan and Waterville, Maine   January 1987 to January 1989
Family Planning Specialist. Provided reproductive health care and crisis counseling.

The Harvard Post, Harvard, Massachusetts   1979 to 1981
Reporter covering women's issues and activities in Harvard and Boston areas.

WRBC Radio, Bates College, Lewiston, Maine   1985 to 1986
WHMB Community Radio, Lewiston, Maine   1985 to 1986
Directed, produced, and announced weekly radio show of women's music.

Bates Student, Bates College, Lewiston, Maine   1983 to 1984
Wrote bi-weekly opinion and events column for student newspaper.

Departmental Assistant, Philosophy and Religion, Bates College, Lewiston   1986 to 1987
Assisted with departmental record-keeping. Performed clerical duties.

SKILLS AND INTERESTS

Fluent in French, both written and spoken. Interests include: music composition and performance, film, literature, visual arts, cycling.

REFERENCES AVAILABLE UPON REQUEST

TARA ANN BETHUNE
511 Northwest Second Avenue
Philadelphia, Pennsylvania 19104
(215) 555-8841

GOAL: To apply my skills and experience with advertising and marketing in a management position.

QUALIFICATIONS:

- Marketing, advertising, sales, graphic productions.
- Records management, including accounts payable/receivable, payroll, inventory control, and tax reporting.
- Purchase of supplies to assure adequate inventories.
- Day-to-day management responsibilities, including scheduling, assigning activities, and program assessments.
- Computer literacy, experience with word processing computer applications.
- Public relations skills, including reception, sales, collections, and purchasing.
- Time management proficiency, promoting timely completion of projects and meeting deadlines.
- Operate wide range of printing and pre-press processing equipment.

EDUCATION:

Community College of Philadelphia, Pennsylvania. 1991-present.
    Business management courses with emphasis in retailing, advertising, marketing, accounting, and human relations. Also completed introductory computer courses.

Philadelphia College of Art, Pennsylvania. 1985-1987.
    Associate of Arts Degree, Process Camera and Stripping.

EXPERIENCE

Management Trainee. Regional School of Ballet, Philadelphia. 1991-1992.
    Duties: Learned and implemented skills in daily management of dance school. Arranged advertising through local media sources. Planned development and marketing strategies. Completed billing reports, payroll records, compiled accounts payable and receivable information. Collected unpaid balances. Ordered and maintained inventories. Supervised staff and scheduled work hours.

Camera Operator/Printer. Sir Speedy Printing, Philadelphia. 1987-1991.
    Duties: Operated variety of camera and bindery equipment, including printer and platemaker. Assisted customers, completed sales transactions and reports, prepared advertising for local media and yellow pages. Began system of tracking advertising results to better determine advertising cost-effectiveness.

Printer. In and Out Printing, Philadelphia. 1987-1989.
    Duties: Operated printing machine and dark-room equipment. Coordinated incoming work assignments. Performed paste-up, platemaking, and bindery duties. Trained newly assigned employees. Composed, printed, and generated monthly newsletter. Carried out projects as assigned.

REFERENCES AVAILABLE UPON REQUEST

Shannon Barker
226 Marquette, #422
Albuquerque, NM 87102
505/555-3119

Objective

A management position in advertising where I can utilize my marketing and management experience.

Work Experience

Seven-Eleven, Albuquerque, NM
Marketing Director, 1990-present
Developed a successful marketing campaign for a convenience store chain. Implemented marketing strategies to increase sales by 23 percent at the least profitable outlets. Initiated and maintained a positive working relationship with radio and print media representatives. Designed a training program for store managers and staff.

Arizona Register, Phoenix, AZ
Advertising Sales, 1986-1990
Sold space advertising to a variety of business and organizational clients. Maintained excellent communications with top clients. Made cold calls on businesses to encourage advertising. Responsible for 25 percent increase in regular advertiser base over four-year period. Coordinated with design and production departments to maintain quality in advertising products as client advocate.

Arizona Evening Herald, Phoenix, AZ
Classified Advertising Sales, 1985-1986.
Sold classified advertising to private and business clients. Entered advertisements in computer system. Checked advertisements for accuracy. Billed clients for advertising. Made follow-up calls to increase run of advertising. Coordinated with advertising department on special issue discount offers in the classified section.

Other work experience includes advertising sales manager for student newspaper, University of Arizona; sales clerk for women's clothing boutique; and sales representative for children's books sold door-to-door.

Education

University of Arizona, Phoenix, AZ
Bachelor of Science in Business, 1985. Major: Advertising and Marketing.
Minor: Communications.
Honors Project Award for Advertising Campaign developed for student newspaper
Dean's Honor Roll
Sigma Delta Gamma, Advertising Honorary

Seminars

Marketing Strategies in Advertising, 1992
Cooperative Advertising: Opportunities for the 1990s, Arizona Press Association, 1989

References available on request

Drew Evan Carlisle
862 Main Street, Apt. 1
Durango, Colorado 81301
(303) 555-2261

Job Objective: A career in the field of advertising.

Experience: <u>Janus Advertising Agency</u>, Boulder, Colorado
Marketing and Sales Assistant, Summer 1991
Assisted Marketing Manager in areas of promotion, product
development, and demographic research and analysis.

<u>TeleMarketing Inc.</u>, Durango, Colorado
Telephone Sales, Summer 1989 and 1990

<u>International House of Pancakes</u>, Durango, Colorado
Waiter and Cashier, June 1988 to June 1991

Education: <u>Fort Lewis College</u>, Durango, Colorado
Bachelor of Arts in Communications, 1992
Major: Advertising. Major GPA: 4.0. Overall GPA: 3.75
Dean's List each semester
Business Club Treasurer
Elected to Student Senate to represent Communications Department
Served on President's Commission for Student Equity

Plan to pursue graduate studies toward a master's degree in advertising
and marketing at Denver University, evening program.

<u>Central High School</u>, Durango, Colorado
Graduated 1987
Top 5 percent of the class
Business manager of student newspaper and student yearbook staffs
Treasurer of Senior Class
Student Council Representative

Special Skills: Fluent in Spanish. Experienced with various computer software and
hardware. Good communications skills.

References: Available upon request

Sujata T. Rao

26 East ThreePenny Road, Detroit, Michigan 33290 / (313) 555-2293 / FAX: (313) 555-2215

Career Objective

Art director for a large Midwest advertising agency.

Career Experience

Bernard Faruch Agency, Detroit, Michigan
Assistant Art Director, 1986 to present
Senior Staff Artist, 1984 to 1986
Staff Artist, 1982 to 1984

Directed creative teams assigned to advertising campaigns. Oversaw all artwork, design, production for print media advertisements. Hired artists, researchers, copywriters, and creative assistants. Conferred with clients and advertising sales managers to determine advertising strategy, market demographics, and positioning. Formulated design concepts. Assigned work to artists, writers, photographers, and production assistants.

Rao and Associates Design, Detroit, Michigan
President and Director, 1978 to 1982

Started graphic design business that attracted a wide variety of clients for production of advertisements for print media. Hired free lance graphic artists, photographers, and copywriters. Worked with clients to determine advertising strategy, audience, and medium. Developed advertising concepts. Prepared camera-ready mechanicals for advertisements, brochures, newsletters, annual reports, flyers, and inserts. Made sales presentations. Worked with various service vendors for typesetting, camera work, pre-press, and printing. Trained new employees in making sales presentations and developing advertising designs to fit a specific marketing strategy or audience.

Education

Museum School, Detroit, Michigan
Graphic Design student, 1976 - 1978

Rhode Island School of Design, Providence, Rhode Island
Graphic Design student, 1975 - 1976

Harvard University, Boston, Massachusetts
Bachelor of Arts in Advertising, 1975

References and portfolio are available on request.

Jameson P. Waterbury III	Work: 212/555-2211
124 West 57th Street	FAX: 212/555-1355
New York, New York 10019	Home: 212/555-2562

Objective: A career in the advertising industry.

Education: **Georgetown University, College of Business,** Washington, D.C.
Bachelor of Arts in Advertising, 1992
Major: Advertising. Minors: Marketing and Graphic Arts.

Skills Development:
- Handled six accounts for mid-sized advertising agency.
- Assisted with traffic control in advertising agency.
- Served as intermediary between client and advertising executives.
- Assisted in writing ad copy and designing ads for magazine publication.
- Sold advertising to various business clients of entertainment weekly.
- Computed ad sizes and ad rates.
- Translated data from dummy to production worksheets.
- Collated editorial and artists' mark-ups to single correction sheet.
- Provided informational assistance to clients.
- Wrote feature articles on local education issues, community events, sports, and arts activities.
- Took photographs in support of articles submitted for publication.

Work Experience: **Johns-Prentice Agency,** New York
- Advertising Intern, Summer 1991

Georgetown Weekend, Washington, D.C.
- Advertising Assistant, part-time 1988-1992

Capitol Reporter, Washington, D.C.
- Freelance Writer, 1990-1992

Honors: Summa Cum Laude, Georgetown University, 1992
Dean's List, 1988-1992
Sullivan Heirs Fellowship in Business
Washington Student Press Corps, Honor Award

References: Provided upon request.

Theresa Vasquez
33528 Santa Monica Boulevard
Los Angeles, California 90088
(213) 555-8842 (days)
(213) 555-3331 (eves)

Career Objective

Traffic manager at an advertising agency or in a corporate advertising department.

Work Experience

Connections Magazine, Hollywood, California
Assistant Production Manager, 1988 to present

Oversee all aspects of production and printing at a national publication. Involved in extensive client and advertising agency contact. Organize all art, mechanicals, and final films with stripping department. Coordinate with editorial and advertising department heads for positioning of advertising. Work with graphic designers on production specifications and proofing. Handle in-depth contact with other media and service vendors. Produce copy and mechanicals for advertisements.

Havener's, Burbank, California
Assistant to Promotion Director, 1984 - 1988

Conducted all in-store promotions and coordinated special events for large department store. Placed advertising and publicity notices in local media. Prepared advertising copy and design mock-ups for promotional ads. Wrote text for radio and television spot announcements. Consulted on grand-opening of Hollywood store. Provided customer assistance.

Trojan, UCLA Student Yearbook, Los Angeles, California
Advertising Manager, 1983 - 1984

Directed advertising sales for 45-page advertising section of student yearbook. Developed sales strategies, assigned territories to sales staff, conducted weekly sales report meetings, tracked sales and billing. Coordinated advertising design and production with graphic design staff. Prepared mock-up ads for sales samples to encourage ad sales for target clients. Developed special ad pages for student advertisements and directed sales efforts.

Education

University of California, Los Angeles
B.S. degree in Advertising and Marketing, 1984

Honors: Cum Laude, 1984; Dean's List, 1982 - 1984; Wilma Morrison Scholarship, 1981 - 1984; National Association of Student Yearbooks, Advertising Sales Award, 1984, Best Advertising Design, 1984.

References provided upon request

Margaret Lawrence

Present Address
2524 Tulsa Hwy
Tulsa, Oklahoma 74115
918/555-8636

Permanent Address
288 Starker Drive
Montgomery, Alabama 36117

Objective:
> To obtain an entry-level position in advertising copywriting.

Education:
> University of Tulsa, Tulsa, Oklahoma
> Expected graduation date, August, 1992. Degree: Bachelor of Arts in advertising with a double minor in journalism and marketing.

Work Experience:

> *PhotoSource,* Tulsa, Oklahoma
> (part-time, August 1991 to present)
>   Advertising space sales
>   Copywriting
>   Order-handling
>   Billing
>   Customer relations

> *The Montgomery Advertiser,* Montgomery, Alabama
> (June 1991 to September 1991)
>   Special studies intern:
>   Design and layout of advertisements
>   Classified ad sales
>   Ad copywriting

Related Coursework:
> Advertising Strategy
> Advertising Copywriting
> Advertising Design
> Advertising Campaign Management
> Public Relations Writing and Research
> Electronic Design and Production
> Marketing for Communication
> Broadcast News Writing

Activities:
> Sigma Delta Chi journalism honorary, Advertising Club, Pi Kappa Phi national sorority, softball team

References
& Portfolio
> Available on request.

ANTHONY J. MAREK   2274 Swanson Place • Hartford, Connecticut 06112
                                                         203.555.2176

OBJECTIVE:

To obtain a position as Art Director, with plenty of challenge and responsibility.

EXPERIENCE:

Creative Advertising Designs, Inc./Hartford   1988 to present
Senior Art Director, Production Manager, Account Executive.

Small advertising/typesetting studio. Responsible for overseeing all projects. Handle all daily business. Supervise three typesetters and four artist/designers. Projects include: print media space advertisements, catalogs, P.O.P., direct mail, consumer, business to business and recruitment advertising with a wide variety of accounts.

Patterson & Associates, Marketing & Advertising Agency/New Haven   1986-1988
Senior Art Director

Managed three-person art department. Supervised layout, design, illustration, and production of consumer, recruitment, and automotive accounts.

Sears Corporation, Corporate Advertising Department/Chicago   1981-1986
Senior Artist, Staff Artist, Production Assistant

Responsibilities included layout, design, illustration, storyboards, and production for corporate headquarters, financial, insurance, and travel sections. Also handled overload from Sears store advertising department.

Freelance Designer/Chicago/New Haven/Hartford   1980-1988

Provided advertisement design, layout, and production for wide range of clients, including newspaper advertising department, automotive dealership, financial organizations, and advertising agencies.

EDUCATION & TRAINING:

Art Institute of Chicago/Illinois
Bachelor of Fine Arts Degree, Graphic Design & Illustration, 1980

How to Buy Printing/Hartford
Two-week seminar on printing specifications, purchasing, and related services.

American Association of Graphic Artists/National
Attended seminars as part of national and regional conventions in areas of electronic pre-press, magazine advertising design, media choices for the 1990s, among others.

AWARDS:

Danny Award, Best Automotive Ad in a Series/Client: Connecticut Buick Dealers Association
Art Institute of Chicago, Design Annual, Honorable Mention

MEMBERSHIPS:

Graphic Design Consortium/Hartford
American Association of Graphic Artists/National

REFERENCES are available upon request

ERIC KRUEGER
2660 N. Fremont
Minneapolis, Minnesota 55440
612.555.5373 (days)
612.555.3954 (eves)

CAREER OBJECTIVE

Seeking a position with an advertising agency that will utilize my skills in computer graphics and desktop publishing.

TECHNICAL SKILLS

Design, layout, production art, illustration, copywriting, editing, typesetting, word processing of magazines, newsletters, display advertisements, flyers, posters, logos, letterheads, business cards, forms, reports, graphs, and other products.

EQUIPMENT/SOFTWARE EXPERIENCE

Compugraphic Editwriter, AM Varityper equipment, IBM and Macintosh computers. WordPerfect, PageMaker, Microsoft Word, Quark XPress, Aldus Freehand, Adobe Illustrator, MacPaint, Corel Draw, Harvard Graphics.

EMPLOYMENT HISTORY

Graphic Communications, St. Paul, Minnesota. 2/86 - 7/92
Chief designer, editor, typesetter for fund raising organization. Prepared posters, designed event-specific logos, produced brochures and other mailing pieces directed at corporate, private, and individual fund raising efforts.

Discount Typesetting, Minneapolis, Minnesota. 11/81 - 1/86
Production artist, typesetter. Copywriter and ad artist for two tabloid and three magazine accounts.

Minneapolis Printing Center, Minneapolis, Minnesota. 6/77 - 11/81
Production artist for fast-service, low-budget printer. Provided clients with typesetting and clip art produced advertising, newsletters, brochures, flyers, tabloids, and other products.

EDUCATION

Northern Illinois University at DeKalb, Illinois
AA 1977. Major: Art/Graphic Design

Truman College, St. Paul, Minnesota
Course work, 1988: Desktop Publishing, Word Processing, Computer Graphics Illustration

American Academy of Art, Chicago, Illinois
Course work, 1975: Computer graphics on the Lumena

AWARDS

First place, student/faculty exhibit, Northern Illinois University
Art editor, *Reflections*, student poetry anthology
Gold Key Awards (Weiboldt Competition)
Summer scholarship at American Academy of Art

References available upon request

WILLIAM L. FINCHLEY JR.

11240 Madison Way • Shreveport, Louisiana 71101 • (318) 555-2485

CAREER OBJECTIVE

To obtain a position as art director for an advertising agency where my skills in design and strategic planning may be effectively utilized.

SKILLS SUMMARY

- Extensive experience in the greeting card industry.
- Key positions include Art Director, Assistant Art Director, Line Planner, and Designer.
- Excellent communication, supervisory, and creative skills.
- Productive professional business attitude and appearance.

PROFESSIONAL EXPERIENCE

Henri Fayette, Inc., Shreveport, LA   March 1982 - Present
Art Director

- Hold complete responsibility for Christmas and special All Occasion card, stationery, and gift lines.
- Participate in corporate strategic planning.
- Plan and balance designs in subject matter and price. Choose paper, operations, and trims.
- Direct staff and work with free lancers.
- Provide press approvals and direct activity of graphic department.
- Revise old dies for new design appearance.
- Design new cards, prepare finished working drawings, die drawings, and cutting samples.
- Choose sentiments, envelopes, and presentation of completed design on mount.

Package Source, Inc., Eureka Division, Shreveport, LA   1979 - 1982
Planner and Designer

- Planned and designed package trims and gift tags.
- Designed and completed finished art for packaging of trims.

Greetings, Inc., Shreveport, LA   1972 - 1978
Head Designer

- Color separator for greeting cards.
- Head designer and line planner for Christmas, all other seasonal lines, and a complete everyday line of greeting cards.
- Coordinated art department projects as assistant to the art director.
- Coordinated projects with advertising department for promotion of special card lines.

ART EDUCATION

McNeese State University, Lake Charles, LA
Associates Degree in Design and Illustration, 1972

References on request

JAMES ANDREW NOVIKYA
3352 W. Sander Drive
Apartment 23
Pittsburgh, PA 28901
412.555-7450

EXPERIENCE:	DESIGN ENGINEER, Palaton Corporation, Pittsburgh, PA Designed and developed product display concepts and illustrated renderings, coordinated computer graphic design orders for client jobs, and responsible for inventory control and product distribution.	May 1991 - present
	DESIGNER, Self-employed Developed concepts and carried them to camera ready state, production, or actual print. Examples of graphic works include book covers, program layout. Also furniture design and interior design consultation. Established clientele and maintained customer service.	June 1988 - present
	GALLERY SUPPORT STAFF, Houston Sutton Galleries, Pittsburgh, PA. Responsible for handling and maintaining works of art before and after sale, upkeep of physical plant and repairs to art works.	March 1990 - May 1991
	MANAGER, Stouffer Street Bar and Grill, Philadelphia, PA. Responsible for banks, scheduling, security, customer service, and payroll.	May 1989 - January 1990
EDUCATION:	Bachelor of Arts, Arts Administration, Andrews University Berrien Springs, MI	May 1989
	Studies in Architectural Design Albright College, Reading, PA	January 1992
AFFILIATIONS:	Progressive Design Group of Pennsylvania Alpha Lambda, Arts Honorary	
SPECIAL SKILLS:	Apple Macintosh design applications: Aldus PageMaker Adobe Illustrator Apple Scan Claris CAD Mac Draw Quark XPress Ultra Paint Virtus Walkthrough Also familiar with general office applications and similar IBM applications.	

REFERENCES AND PORTFOLIO AVAILABLE UPON REQUEST

Stuart G. Swanson
1644 Howard Street
Pontiac, MI 48057
616/555-1197

OBJECTIVE: *To join the advertising and promotion department of a large arts organization where my skills in arts marketing and graphic design may be directed toward advertising and fundraising projects.*

EDUCATION: *Master of Arts, Arts Administration,* December 1990
Sangamon State University, Springfield, IL
G.P.A. 3.9
Relevant Courses:

Arts Administration	Organizational Dynamics
Marketing	Museum Management
Fundraising	Financial Management
Public Policy	Legal Aspects
Research Methods	

Bachelor of Science, Art, May 1989
University of Wisconsin, Madison, WI
G.P.A. 3.4; Dean's List, 1988-1989
Relevant Courses:

Painting	Drawing
Printmaking	Graphic Design
Typography	Computer Art
Numerous Art History courses	

EXPERIENCE:

1990 *Michigan Arts Board, Percent for Art Program, Pontiac, MI*
Program Assistant
Δ Designed flyers, posters, and advertisements announcing competitions
Δ Served as administrative assistant to public art program coordinator
Δ Researched other public art programs for policy development purposes
Δ Prepared detailed reports on the program's operational effectiveness
Δ Systematized slide registry and project files
Δ Assisted in art and artist selection procedures
Δ Coordinated selection committee meetings and slide presentations
Δ Served as communication link between director, artists, and committees

1989-1990 *Michigan Art-in-Architecture Program, Detroit, MI*
Intern
Δ Served as an intern for the public art program
Δ Designed and produced a collection brochure
Δ Wrote text for brochures and catalog
Δ Assembled slide presentations and updated project files
Δ Assisted in selection committee meetings
Δ Assisted with framing and delivery of art work

1987-1989 *Duradata, Inc., Madison, WI*
Laser Printer Operator
Δ Served as operator of computer source laser printers
Δ Designed logos and forms using IBM/Xerox/Intran combination
Δ Produced and distributed laser print and microfiche
Δ Some programming and troubleshooting of laser printers

REFERENCES: Provided upon request.

Trevor Ghering
323 South Whitelaw
Atlanta, Georgia 30316
404/555-8846

Designer/Illustrator   *Atlanta, GA*   *1972 to present*

Operate free lance business interacting directly with publishers, agencies, manufacturers, distributors, film and slide producers, and entrepreneurs.

Client Contact

As consulting art director, confer with clients to interpret the design problem and involve them on design approaches. Establish budget perimeters. Determine illustrative needs. Advise on reproduction methods.

Creativity

Conceptualize design solution. Produce layouts translating clients' information into display form. Select typography, color, illustrations, photography, and other imaging.

Production

Supervise typesetting, photography, or other specialized arts as needed. Produce finished keyline art for reproduction. Coordinate with printers and other service bureaus for production of finished product.

Experience

Design ↑ Produce work for print and film advertisements, brochure literature, books, publications, catalogs, posters, logos, trademarks, annual reports, labels and packages, slide programs, animated sequences, and games.

Illustration

Produce illustration for client projects with both traditional methods and computerized graphics software. Products illustrated include educational , technical, symbolic, humorous, whimsical, and traditional.

Education

Bachelor of Fine Arts, Graphic Design
California College of Arts and Crafts, Oakland, CA
Degree awarded 1972

Additional study, Computer Graphics
Atlanta College of Art, Atlanta, GA
Post-baccalaureate study, 1988 to 1990

References and portfolio available on request

AURELIA LANAE BARKER
223 West 104th
New York, NY 10025
212/555-2776

OBJECTIVE   Seeking a position as account executive in a small advertising firm.

EXPERIENCE

4/91-   New York Pharmacists Association   New York, NY
State Pharmaceutical Editorial Association Administrative Manager
Serve as liaison between pharmaceutical advertising agencies and 19 State
Pharmaceutical journals. In charge of all ad placements and ad rates. Develop,
organize, and implement media mailing list, SPEA rate card, media kits. Handle all
bookkeeping and billing.

3/89-4/91   *Communications Assistant*
Desktop publishing, typesetting and paste-up of monthly pharmaceutical
journal. Used IBM-compatible computer and software such as Aldus PageMaker,
Micrographix Designer, Adobe TypeAlign, Picture Publisher, Photo Styler, Word
Perfect 5.0. Organized and purchased all public relations materials, programs,
and services for members.

1988-1989   Our Saviors Church   Brooklyn, NY
Print Manager
Designed and printed all brochures, bulletins, and programs. Ordered all
supplies needed for print room operations. Supervised print shop operations
and maintained budget, supplemented by performing work for outside clients
during slack production times. Managed staff of three full-time and six part-time
workers.

1986-88   Diversified Home Services   Brooklyn, NY
Telemarketing Manager
Responsible for hiring and training employees. Implemented monthly, weekly
and daily reports. Handled payroll. Rated highest personal sales and office
volume in the entire corporation. Awarded numerous sales, volume, and
motivational awards.

EDUCATION

1988   City College, New York
Graphic Design, Bachelor of Arts

1984-86   Brooklyn College, Brooklyn, New York
Business Major

References available on request

Christine Westerburg
222 Joslyn Street, N.W.
Seattle, Washington 98012
(206) 555-1223

Objective	To obtain a position as an assistant advertising executive.

Achievements

- Coordinated media planning and buying
- Researched potential markets for ad campaigns
- Supervised artwork, layout, and production
- Handled sales promotions
- Supervised trade shows and press shows
- Arranged and conducted sales meetings and presentations
- Designed and distributed press packets
- Developed marketing strategies
- Planned marketing and advertising campaigns
- Wrote and distributed press releases
- Served as liaison between clients and media representatives
- Acted as liaison to outside advertising agencies

Work Experience

Advertising Coordinator, 1990-present
RHB Furniture Design Center, Seattle

Assistant Coordinator of Advertising, 1985-1989
Nordstrom, Central Office, Seattle

Assistant Sales Manager, 1983-1984
Nordstrom, Bellevue

Salesperson, 1982-1983
Nordstrom, Bellevue

Education

Bachelor of Arts, English
University of Washington, 1981

Seminars

"Mail Order and Direct Mail Advertising," University of Washington Business Center
"Account Management," Seattle University Summer Program, Continuing Education

References

Available on request.

Yuri T. Lobojko
2245 South Lawn
Los Angeles, California 90016
(213) 555-9197 (D)
(213) 555-2983 (E)

Career Objective: Advertising Director for a television station.

Skills & Achievements

Promotion and Marketing

* Wrote and designed advertisements of various lengths and short promotional spots
* Evaluated content and direction of station promotions
* Handled market research/demographic studies
* Consulted station managers and executives on marketing strategies

Video Production and Editing

* Supervised shooting procedures, audio, lighting, casting, and editing
* Wrote and edited scripts for advertisements and two 30-minute public service documentaries
* Determined production values for marketing accounts
* Oversaw post-production and placement
* Coordinated presentations to clients

Media Planning and Management

* Advised clients on media strategies
* Oversaw media budgets
* Determined and implemented marketing objectives
* Oversaw strategic planning sessions
* Supervised design teams
* Negotiated spot rates for clients

Related Employment

Trumball Advertising, Hollywood, California
Media Planner, 1987 - 1992

Starnes and Starnes, Inc., San Diego, California
Assistant Media Buyer, 1981 - 1986

KQRY Radio FM, San Francisco, California
Advertising Assistant, 1979-1981

Education

University of Southern California, Los Angeles
Bachelor of Arts in Business; Minor in Film/Video Production
Degree awarded 1980
Graduated cum laude
Awarded second place in USC Filmmakers Annual, 1980; honorable mention, 1979

References are available on request.

Gil Sanders
221 West Ventura Boulevard
Santa Monica, California 90403
818/555-7452

Career Objective	Traffic manager for an advertising agency that will utilize my creativity, organization, and communication skills to advantage.

Experience

* Oversaw all aspects of production and printing at a national publication.

* Actively involved in client and agency communications.

* Organized all art, mechanicals, and final films with stripping department.

* Handled in-depth media background contact with other media.

* Conducted all in-store promotions and events for the state's largest bookstore.

* Produced copy for ads.

* Placed advertising and publicity in local publications.

* Worked as operations director for small mail order company.

Work History

Broad Horizons Magazine, Santa Monica, California
Assistant to the Production Manager, 1988 - present

Radio Shack, Inc., Corporate Headquarters, San Francisco, California
Assistant to the Promotion/Advertising Director, 1984 - 1987

Education

Bachelor of Arts, Business Administration, 1984
Minor: Advertising
University of California at Santa Cruz

Seminar: "Time and Resources Management" 1988
Workshop: "Production and Printing Innovations" 1991

Honors

Reedmore Scholarship, 1982-1984
Dean's List, 1982-1984
Best Undergraduate Project, UCSC Honors College

References

Available on request

PARKER ALLEN
334 Market Avenue
St. Louis, Missouri 53190
313-555-2468

OBJECTIVE

A career in advertising media services where I can utilize my skills in marketing, organization, and communication.

EDUCATION

University of Missouri, Kansas City. Degree awarded June 1992.
B.A. in Advertising
Major field G.P.A.: 3.75
G.P.A. overall: 3.45

Honors & Activities:
Honors College graduate
Business Representative to Associated Student Government
Chair, Honors Curriculum Student Committee
Student Representative, College of Business Promotion and Tenure Committee
Officer, African-American Students Cultural Association

WORK EXPERIENCE

Markham Advertising, Kansas City, MO.
Advertising Intern, Summer 1991

Worked with advertising account executive and marketing manager in the areas of promotion, product development, market research, and demographic analysis. Through research and market analysis, identified prime prospects for target advertising. Coordinated production of a series of target advertisements directed at college students for a client who operated a local recreation organization. Received highest possible ratings for internship.

Big River Marketing, Kansas City, MO.
Telemarketing Salesperson, 1988 - 1991

Missouri Highway Department, St. Louis, MO.
Flagger/Driver, Road Construction Crew, Summers 1988 - 1990

SPECIAL SKILLS

Working knowledge of Spanish and Italian. Experienced with several computer software programs for data entry and analysis. Completed special projects on media services and advertising market research for corporate and nonprofit organizations.

References available as requested.

Xin Quon
66 Western Boulevard
Houston, Texas 75733
(713) 555-8844

Objective   A career in radio advertising sales and customer service.

Experience   WRNK-Radio AM, Houston, Texas
Intern, Advertising Department, January to June, 1992
(Three months in sales, three months in production)

• Made cold calls on business clients to sell advertising spots.
• Added nine new first-time clients in three-month sales internship period.
• Produced public service announcement segments for play during evening news hour.
• Wrote advertising copy for local clients.
• Auditioned and selected actors and musicians for producing commercial spots.
• Worked with technicians to produce local commercial spots.
• Assisted advertising sales staff with record-keeping and sales reports.

WESU-Radio FM, East Texas State University, Commerce, Texas
Advertising Manager, September 1989 to December 1991

• Directed sales staff in radio advertising sales.
• Developed sales program that increased ad income by 15%.
• Produced radio ads, from concept to finished ad.
• Programmed advertising for 12-hour shift.
• Figured ad rates and scheduled discounts.
• Handled all billing and bookkeeping.
• Worked with station manager and adviser on annual budgeting.
• Produced top 40 hit music show for radio.
• Served as announcer for twice-monthly student government program.

Education   B.A. in Communications, with emphasis on Radio and Television Media
Minor: Business Administration and Advertising
East Texas State University, Commerce, Texas
Degree awarded 1992. Major G.P.A., 3.89. Overall G.P.A. 3.2.
Dean's List
Texas Young Broadcasters Association
Ad Club, Vice President, 1991

References   Available upon request.

JEFFREY SCOTT WINSTON JR.
225 Melrose Park Lane
Savannah, Georgia 30290

912/555-3324

EDUCATION

Savannah University, Savannah, Georgia   **M.S. in Communications, 1992**

Relevant coursework: advertising in print media, advertising in radio, advertising in television, public relations, career ad copywriting, marketing research methods, strategic methods in advertising and public relations, management, behavioral communications, statistical methods

Research project: Advertising sales strategies and results in five urban and five rural radio stations, controlled for staff and budget resources.

University of Nevada, Las Vegas   **B.S. in Journalism/Advertising, 1990**

Relevant coursework: ad copywriting, public relations, communications media, reporting, history of advertising and the media, storyboarding, visual presentation strategies (seminar)

EXPERIENCE

Sophronia Digest, Savannah, Georgia   **Summer Advertising Intern, 1991**

Served in advertising sales. Wrote sales letters to established and potential clients, notifying them of special issues and deadline dates. Received and catalogued camera-ready ads for placement in magazine. Worked with advertising design department to develop concepts and copy for self-promotion advertisements. Assisted with office management and billing.

University of Nevada, Las Vegas   **Research/Office Assistant, 1989-1991**

Served School of Journalism as research assistant and office assistant. Worked with faculty on media research projects. Assisted with data entry, statistical analysis, and documentation. Assisted with editing of quarterly alumni newsletter. Prepared and sent bulk mailings. Gained experience with IBM and Macintosh desktop publishing and communications software and statistical analysis software used in media research.

HONORS & ACTIVITIES

Journalism Honorary, Sigma Delta Chi
Advertising Associates, Secretary, 1989-1990
Marshfield Scholarship for Journalism
Dean's List, 1988-1990

REFERENCES AVAILABLE ON REQUEST

TERRENCE BULEIGH

▲ JOB OBJECTIVE

A management position in cable television advertising sales where my skills in planning, strategy, and sales can be utilized to increase sales revenue.

▲ RELEVANT EXPERIENCE

△ Sold space in television for four major clients in the automotive industry.

△ Served as liaison between clients and television and radio salespeople.

△ Bought local television and radio advertising space for large retail department store.

△ Sold space for daytime programming on local television station.

△ Advised station manager on content and suitability of advertisements and potential liability.

△ Worked with creative departments to develop advertisement concepts for potential clients.

▲ WORK HISTORY

△ AdMedia Agency, Providence, RI
　Space Sales, Broadcast Media Division
　October 1988 - present

△ WVIR Television Station, Bangor, ME
　Television Space Sales
　June 1985 - September 1988

△ KQRX Radio FM, Eugene, OR
　Staff Sales Assistant, Advertising Department
　June 1983 - April 1985

▲ EDUCATION

　Broadcast Media, B.A. 1983
　Oregon State University, Corvallis, OR

　△ Honors:
　　Best Senior Project, Broadcast Media Communications Department, 1983
　　Dean's List, 1981 - 1983
　　Rijken Junior Scholarship in Broadcast Media, 1982

References provided upon request

819 JOHNSON PARKWAY ▲ PROVIDENCE RI 02803 ▲ (401) 555-3461

Franklin Jordan Andrews
66 Traver Lane
Lincoln, Nebraska 68508
402/555-1967
FAX: 402/555-3375

Job Objective

Position as Advertising Manager for large national corporation. Willing to relocate.

Employment History

Director of Operations, Outdoor Life Magazine, Lincoln, NE, 1988 to present
Supervised 22 regional managers and offices with 385 employees. Oversaw all central office operations, including circulation, advertising sales, promotion and marketing, and $25 million budget administration. Developed and implemented new advertising sales management team, which produced a 20% increase in ad sales revenue over two years.

Assistant to General Manager, Outdoor Life Magazine, Lincoln, NE, 1984 - 1988
Coordinated all of the magazine's configuration changes. Served as operations liaison to the European edition of Outdoor Life. Initiated subscription sales programs and formulated marketing strategies. Increased sales of subscription mailing lists through target advertising campaign. Developed and implemented several edition modifications to boost circulation sales and optimize advertising revenue.

Advertising Manager, Sunset Magazine, Menlo Park, CA, 1977 - 1984
Directed operations of five regional offices, with a sales staff of 84 and 35 support staff. Served as liaison with general management. Developed new advertising sections in order to target ad sales. Boosted advertising revenue base by $7.5 million over three years.

Regional Sales Manager, Sunset Magazine, Seattle, WA 1975 - 1977
Met with corporate advertising representatives to coordinate strategy and make sales presentations. Worked closely with corporate advertisers to plan space acquisition and optimal presentations.

Advertising Sales Representative, Sunset Magazine, Seattle, WA 1973 - 1975
Handled six major national corporate accounts. Coordinated advertising sales team in regional office. Developed sales presentations for special advertising sections. Brought in several new corporate clients over two-and-a-half year period.

Media Buyer, Julian Friedan Advertising Agency, Boston, MA, 1970 - 1972
Served as media liaison between corporate clients and media sales representatives. Purchased space advertising in newspapers, magazines, radio, and television, including cable and network t.v. Devised timetables and strategies in conjunction with media research and market analysis reports. Negotiated ad rates and discounts for corporate clients.

Media Research, World Magazine, Amherst, MA, 1968 - 1970
Tracked market changes, with responsibility for preparing reports on significant developments and potential for impact on advertising sales. Worked with advertising sales department on developing demographic data.

F. J. Andrews - 2

Education

M.B.A., University of Washington, Seattle, WA, 1973

B.S., University of Massachusetts, Amherst, MA 1968

Professional Memberships

West Coast Magazine Publishers Association
National Association of Magazine Publishers
International Association of Business Communicators
International Advertisers Association

References are provided upon request.

Samuel J. Barstow
132 S. Pennsylvania Ave.
Washington, D.C. 02165
202-555-3364
Message: 202-555-7736

Objective: A career in advertising.

Work History:

On Broadway Magazine, New York, NY
Assistant Production Manager, 1986 - 1992

Oversaw all aspects of production and printing at the central office. Worked closely with advertising sales and clients on advertising placement and scheduling. Organized all art, mechanicals and final film with stripping department. Produced copy for advertisements.

Market Start, Washington, D.C.
Assistant to Promotion Director, 1982 - 1986

Worked with promotion director to plan in-store promotions and events. Coordinated all activities in preparation for events. Purchased advertising space to promote events and special promotions. Worked with graphic designers to develop banners, posters, flyers, and advertisements. Wrote advertising copy. Scheduled special celebrity guests and made arrangements for their travel and hospitality.

Education: Georgetown University, Washington, D.C.
B.S. in Communications, 1982

Relevant coursework: advertising, promotions and public relations, advertising copywriting, public relations writing, marketing and sales, strategic planning

Activities: Business and Advertising Society, Chair of Campus Cultural Diversity Task Force, Chamber Music Ensemble, Georgetown University Symphony Orchestra

References: Available on request.

| ALEISHA | 445 S. Magnolia | 504/555-4485 |
| CLARKE | Baton Rouge, Louisiana 20928 | 504/555-2469 |

CAREER OBJECTIVE

Advertising sales assistant position where I can effectively utilize my background in advertising, marketing, and sales.

EDUCATION

<u>University of Louisiana</u>, Baton Rouge
Bachelor of Arts, Advertising   1992

Major Fields: Advertising, Marketing, Public Relations, Business Management

HONORS

Summa Cum Laude, 1992
Dean's List
Advertising Senior Award for Best Ad Campaign
International Newspaper Advertising and Marketing Executives First Award
Honors in Advertising, American Advertising Federation, National Student Advertising Competition

WORK EXPERIENCE

<u>Rouge et Noire, Inc.</u>, Baton Rouge, LA
Advertising Intern, Summer 1991
Handled three accounts for advertising agency. Worked with designers to develop ad concepts and designs. Wrote ad copy. Assisted with traffic control. Met with clients to discuss marketing strategy and target markets. Served as intermediary between client and account executives.

<u>University of Louisiana</u>, Baton Rouge, LA
Advertising Manager, Yearbook Staff, 1990 - 1992
Supervised advertising sales staff for yearbook. Coordinated sales of 22 pages of advertising. Met with corporate and individual clients to make sales presentations. Worked with design staff to develop advertisements. Wrote ad copy. Assisted with production of final ads. Distributed proof copies for review and approval from clients. Provided informational assistance to clients and yearbook manager. Exceeded budget projections for advertising sales revenue.

REFERENCES

Provided upon request

JAMILLA STEWART-LAWRENCE

PRESENT ADDRESS:
125 W. Hollis Ave., No. 6
Charlotte, NC 28230
(704) 555-2789

PERMANENT ADDRESS:
556 E. Marquette St.
Richmond, VA 18975

JOB OBJECTIVE: To obtain a challenging position in a dynamic work environment, which requires skills in advertising, sales, writing, and promotions.

EDUCATION: <u>Bachelor of Arts, Broadcast Journalism and Advertising</u>
June, 1992, University of North Carolina, Charlotte
Minor: Psychology

EXPERIENCE: <u>Advertising/Public Relations Intern</u>
University Savings Bank, Charlotte, North Carolina
April to June 1992
Developed and implemented promotional ideas. Created, designed, and composed advertising copy and graphics on desktop publishing system. Served as assistant editor of employee newsletter.

<u>Advertising Campaign</u>
Advanced Advertising Project, University of North Carolina
Fall 1991
Assisted in the creation of a new Perrier campaign designed to position the product against the diet soft drink industry. Campaign selected by Perrier Corporation for implementation. Fall 1991

<u>Resident Adviser</u>
University of North Carolina, Charlotte
September to June, 1988 to 1991
Developed and promoted more than 20 programs dealing with current issues in education, culture, religion, and health. Selected to edit campus residence hall newsletter.

<u>Television/Radio Intern</u>
WIRO-TV, WIRE News Radio, Richmond, Virginia
Summer, 1991
Independently wrote more than 50 advertisement spots and public service announcements, working with clients. Updated and revised advertising prospects file. Worked with advertising sales crew to develop sales strategies. Made sales calls with sales representatives.

ACHIEVEMENTS: Outstanding Performance Award, University Savings Bank
Alumni Relations Chairperson, Gamma Phi Beta Sorority
Executive Council Member, Gamma Phi Beta
Leadership Camp Director, Sullivan Forest, Virginia

REFERENCES: Provided on request.

Reece Hartshore

1986 21st Avenue S.E. • Manhattan, KS 66502 (316) 555-8552

Professional Goal

To obtain an entry-level position with a dynamic advertising agency.

Experience

- Developed and implemented promotional ideas.
- Assisted with development of national advertising campaign.
- Worked with strategy team to develop new product position.
- Created, designed, and composed advertising copy and graphics.
- Trained on desktop publishing and computer graphics software.
- Made advertising sales calls to prospective radio advertising clients.
- Wrote advertising copy for radio commercial spots.
- Worked with advertising sales department to increase client base.
- Wrote and edited company newsletter.
- Received outstanding performance award for distinguished work.
- Served as alumni relations coordinator for national fraternity.
- Developed and promoted educational and cultural programs.

Education

- Bachelor of Science, Business, 1990
  Duke University, Durham, NC

Work History

- WROC-FM, Radio, Manhattan, KS, 1992-present
  Advertising Sales Associate

- Bank of North Carolina, Durham, NC, 1990-1992
  Assistant to the Vice President for Advertising and Promotions

References are available on request

Duncan Stuart McPherson
3359 Potter Avenue East
Boston, Mass. 02115
602/555-2956

Job Objective: Advertising copywriting position.

Education:

   Bachelor of Arts, Journalism and Advertising
   March 1990, University of Massachusetts
   Minor: Public Relations Writing

Employment and Relevant Experience:

Advertising/Public Relations Writing

 - Editor and writer for employee newsletter, BankNotes
   Massachusetts First Bank, Boston
   April 1990 - present

Developed and coordinated promotional events and campaigns.
Created, designed and wrote copy for institutional
advertisements. Produced ads on desktop publishing software
on IBM-compatible computer.

 - Intern, Advertising and Marketing Department
   Crystal Springs, Boston
   Summer 1989

Developed marketing strategy and complete print media
advertising campaign for local bottled water company as part
of class project. Campaign was adapted for use in four
eastern states.

Promotions

 - Residence Hall Assistant Director
   University of Massachusetts, Boston
   1987 - 1989

Developed and promoted speakers forum and group discussions
on topics ranging from race relations to AIDS. Scheduled
visits from professionals in the city to make presentations
to student organizations. Handled all promotion and
publicity for the events, which developed a large campus
following.

Duncan Stuart McPherson - 2

News Writing

- Intern, News Department
  WBMG Radio News
  Summer 1988

Independently wrote over 50 broadcast news stories. Updated and revised reporter's stories. Developed skills in interviewing and research techniques. Assisted with writing of advertising spots and public service announcements. Exercised editorial judgment in story selection and order of presentation during news segment.

Achievements and Memberships:

Dean's List, University of Massachusetts
Merit Award, Spot News Story, BYBA Annual 1991
Boston Young Broadcasters Association
Sigma Delta Chi, Journalism Honorary
Massachusetts Writers Collective

References are available on request.

Jorje Alcalá   513/555-2896
224 E. 14th Street   513/555-9824
Cincinnati, OH   (message)

JOB OBJECTIVE: Media planning position with an advertising agency.

SKILLS AND ACHIEVEMENTS

Media Planning

* Headed strategic planning team that handled twelve major corporate accounts
* Advised clients on media strategies
* Consulted with clients on marketing goals and helped translate into specific
    action-oriented plans
* Oversaw media budgets and authorized space advertising purchases
* Determined and implemented marketing objectives
* Consulted with corporate clients on market segment and demographics research
    analysis
* Negotiated spot rates and frequency discounts for corporate clients

Promotion and Marketing

* Wrote and designed promotional pieces for distribution to media
* Evaluated content and direction of promotional campaigns
* Handled market research, demographic research, and analysis
* Made sales presentations to clients

EMPLOYMENT HISTORY

Sarton Advertising, Inc., Cincinnati, OH
Associate Media Planner, 1991 - present

Graves and Albright, Ltd., Cleveland, OH
Assistant Media Buyer, 1988 - 1991

Macy's, Chicago, IL
Advertising Assistant, 1986 - 1988

EDUCATION

Capital University, Columbus, OH
B.A. in Economics, 1986
Minor in Advertising

REFERENCES AVAILABLE

DAMONE X. WILSON
3340 W. Moreno St. Apt. 17 • Rutland, VT 05701 • (802) 555-2948

JOB SOUGHT: Management position in the advertising department of a major food manufacturing company.

RELEVANT
EXPERIENCE: <u>Management</u>

• Managed sales/marketing staff which included advertising account managers and sales representatives.
• Monitored and studied the effectiveness of a national distribution and marketing network.
• Oversaw all aspects of sales and marketing budget.

<u>Advertising</u>

• Represented company to advertising agencies and retailers in order to develop advertising strategies for new products.
• Organized and planned convention displays and strategies.
• Designed and executed direct mail advertising campaign that identified market needs and new options for products.

<u>Development</u>

• Conceived ads, posters, and displays for point-of-purchase sales in department store and grocery store chains.
• Initiated and published monthly newsletter that was distributed to current and potential retailers.

EMPLOYMENT
HISTORY: <u>Maple Confections</u>, Rutland, VT
National Sales Manager, 1987 - present
Account Manager, 1985 - 1987
Assistant Account Manager, 1984 - 1985
Sales Assistant, 1982 - 1984

EDUCATION: B.A. in English, 1981
Northwestern University, Evanston, IL

SEMINARS: American Marketing Association Seminars, 1985 - 1992
Product Positioning: Strategies and Planning, 1989
Media Options: What You Get for Your Media Dollar, 1988

REFERENCES: Available on request

Angela Fuentes
2120 Market, Apt. 14
Dallas, Texas 73389
206-555-2004

Career Objective

Advertising assistant position where I can utilize my skills in organization, planning, and writing.

Employment History

Dallas Senior Center, Dallas, Texas
Administrative Assistant to Director of Public Relations, 1988 - present

Write and distribute news releases about center events, educational programs, and issues. Maintained personal media contacts. Prepare and edit copy for advertisements, brochures, posters, and public service radio announcements. Develop advertising schedule and negotiate space rates and frequency discounts for print and radio advertising. Coordinate special events programming and implement plans. Handle all booking for live entertainment. Prepare and distribute newsletter to patrons.

Center for Personal Growth, Dallas, Texas
Office Manager, 1985 - 1988

Coordinated workshops and seminars for continuing education program. Taught workshop on obtaining free publicity for local events. Supervised an office staff of eight. Coordinated all travel and hospitality arrangements for visiting dignitaries. Maintained business calendar. Organized staff meetings. Made all arrangements for national convention. Prepared monthly financial reports. Handled payroll and supervised bookkeeping and budgeting functions.

Education

Dallas Christian College, Dallas, Texas, 1984
B.A. in English with a minor in Psychology

Special Skills

Typing, 75 wpm; dictation, bookkeeping, word processing, computer graphics

References

Provided on request

Han So Wan
Illustration • Photography • Design • Production
200 Wimmer Blvd.
LaJolla, CA 94340
619/555-4975

Career Objective

Commercial artist for an advertising agency.

Skills & Accomplishments

- Produced line drawings for magazine advertisements, 35mm slides, and promotional materials.
- Experienced in watercolors, acrylics, air brush techniques, and pastels.
- Handled all aspects of production, from concept to finished mechanicals.
- Experienced with 35mm color and black and white photography. Own Leica professional equipment and have extensive lighting facilities for studio shooting.
- Some experience with film stripping, trapping, and masking.

Employment History

La Jolla Productions, Inc., La Jolla, CA
- Commercial Artist, Summers 1990 to present

University of New Mexico, Albuquerque, NM
- Staff Photographer, Department of Printing, 1990 to 1991 (school year)

Coleman College, La Mesa, CA
- Assistant, Design Department, Summers 1988 to 1989

Education

University of New Mexico, Albuquerque, NM
- BFA in Illustration and Painting; minor in photography, 1992

References

Available on request

Tanya Welsh
2235 N. Oak Street
Iowa City, Iowa 52240
(319) 555-5892

CAREER
OBJECTIVE
An entry-level position in the field of advertising, preferably in the area of market research.

EDUCATION
UNIVERSITY OF IOWA, Iowa City, IA
B.S. degree in advertising with minor in marketing, expected December 1993
GPA: 3.5 (overall)/4.0 (major field)

Pertinent courses:

Advertising	Public Relations
Marketing Management	Industrial Marketing
Research Methods	Business Statistics
Marketing Research	Advertising Campaigns
Consumer Behavior	

EXPERIENCE
UNIVERSITY OF IOWA, College of Business
Research Assistant, 1988 to present

o Conduct surveys under diverse conditions and among varied consumer groups, including college students, retail store and motion picture patrons, and heads of households.

o Compile data from various studies to form basis for a national research project on consumer spending potential for leisure products.

o Write summary reports on findings, including preliminary analysis.

THE DAILY IOWAN, University of Iowa Student Newspaper
Advertising Manager

o Increased the number of regular advertisers from 12 to 22 over a period of three semesters.

o Eliminated paper's budget deficit through increased advertising revenue.

o Handled budgeting and payroll for staff of four commission sales representatives.

ACTIVITIES
American Advertising Association member, student chapter
Treasurer, Key Club, Service Honorary
Marching Band

References are available on request

Dai Guillame
261 West First
Brooklyn, NY 11221   Telephone: (212) 555-2294

Objective
Seeking an entry-level position in advertising/marketing, with opportunity for advancement. Willing to relocate anywhere in the U.S. or overseas.

Academic Summary
Adelphi University, Garden City, New York
B.S. Advertising, Minor: Marketing and Public Relations
June 1992; GPA 3.2 (4.0)
Dean's List, five semesters

Relevant Experience

Brooklyn Borough Chamber of Commerce (Work Experience, Spring 1992)
• Worked with advertising agency to develop advertising campaign to promote corporate employment training opportunities.
• Designed two posters used for promoting industrial development opportunities.
• Wrote copy for public service announcements for radio and cable television.
• Recruited speakers for monthly Chamber meetings.
• Coordinated and distributed meeting agendas.
• Assisted Chamber Director in promoting organization's activities.

Small Business Administration (Internship, sponsored by Advertising Department, Adelphi University, Summer 1991), Garden City, New York
• Conducted demographics study of small businesses in Upstate New York.
• Presented study findings to Garden City Chamber of Commerce.
• Wrote summary report on study results, published in New York Business magazine.
• Wrote copy for, designed, and produced a pamphlet on services provided by the SBA for small business operators.

Public Relations and Development Office, Brooklyn General Hospital (Internship, Summer 1989)
• Prepared layout and edited text for three issues of General News, 8-page hospital newsletter for medical and support staff.
• Prepared community service advertisements for local newspapers to promote health care courses offered through the hospital.
• Attended seminar on hospital public relations programs.

HOPE (Volunteer for nonprofit organization that helps handicapped individuals find employment, 1990 to present)
• Wrote press releases and public service announcements to seek employment opportunities and announce available services to qualified individuals.
• Worked with management personnel to develop promotional strategies for reaching handicapped individuals.

Awards and Activities
• Certificate of Merit, Small Business Administration
• Certificate of Appreciation, Brooklyn Borough Chamber of Commerce
• Secretary, Marketing Club, Adelphi University
• Member, Lambda Beta Honorary

References
On file with Adelphi University Placement Office, and available on request.

Angelique Brady
88 Park Lane
Baltimore, Maryland 21206   Telephone: (301) 555-2984

Job Objective: To work in an advertising design position that will utilize
my creativity, visual organization, and communication skills.

Education: <u>University of Illinois</u>, College of Fine and Applied Arts,
Urbana-Champaign, Urbana, IL
Bachelor of Fine Arts in Industrial Design, May 1991

<u>Relevant Courses</u>: Design Studio, Design Methodology,
Materials Processing, Rendering, AutoCAD, Practical
Physics, Advertising, and Photography.

<u>Activities</u>: Affiliate member, Industrial Designers Society of
America

**Employment
Experience:**   1991 to present   <u>Brightwood Temporary Services</u>
Baltimore, Maryland
* Accounts payable assistant
* Chartered microfilmed invoices
* Route sales auditor

Summer & Winter   <u>Affiliated Bank of Baltimore</u>
Breaks, 1987 to   Baltimore, Maryland
1992   * Bank teller
* Managed currency, balanced figures
* Data entry; used CRT daily
* Direct customer interaction

Honors: Finalist, Baltimore Designers Guild Annual Competition
Works exhibited at Krannert Art Museum, Urbana-Champaign
and Baltimore Designers Guild Gallery
Dean's List, four semesters

References: On request

Gillian K. Robinson

Current Address:	**Permanent Address:**
1100 E. Grand, 16-5B	55 W. Third Ave.
Bloomington, Indiana 42167	Houston, Texas 77054
(812) 555-6724	(713) 555-5876

Objective

To obtain an advertising sales position with opportunities for advancement in the field of publishing.

Education

INDIANA UNIVERSITY, Bloomington, IN
Bachelor of Arts, Advertising with Minor in English
Anticipated December 1993. Current GPA 3.93/4.0

REND LAKE COLLEGE, Ina, IL
Associate of Arts, English
December 1988. GPA 3.94/4.0

Honors

INDIANA UNIVERSITY
* Selma Jane Rockfield Scholarship, IU College of Business
* Jefferson County Alumni Association Scholarship
* Admissions and Records Academic Scholarship
* Dean's List

REND LAKE COLLEGE
* President's Scholarship
* Benton Business and Professional Women's Club Scholarship
* President's Honor List

Activities

INDIANA UNIVERSITY
* Sigma Tau Delta, Advertising Honorary, Treasurer
* Member, Phi Kappa Phi, National Honorary
* Member, College of Business Honor Society
* Advertising Club, Membership Secretary

REND LAKE COLLEGE
* Member, Phi Theta Kappa
* Student Delegate, Rend Lake College #521 Board of Trustees
* Student Representative, Campus and Facilities Committee
* Illinois Governmental Internship Program

Work History

INDIANA UNIVERSITY
<u>Tutor</u>, Achievement Plus Program, 8/90 to present
* Tutored learning disabled college students in English.
* Assisted in drafting, editing, and proofing essays.

<u>Student Secretary</u>, Chair, Dept. of Curriculum and Instruction, 1/89 to present
* Involved in word processing on IBM and Apple computers.
* Completed proofreading, editing, revising, and drafting of departmental documents and correspondence.

REND LAKE COLLEGE
<u>Student Assistant</u>, Registrar/Admissions Office, 9/87 to 6/88
* Performed computer data entry, student registration processing, and maintenance of student transcripts.
* Created and maintained correspondence and official documents.

Additional

Willing to travel and relocate. References on request.

CONFIDENTIAL RESUME

Brian Bassist
1134 Valley Road
Flint, Michigan 62340
(606) 555-2849 (office)
(606) 555-1003 (home)

Objective

Partner in advertising agency specializing in corporate advertising.

Education

Masters in Business Administration, Advertising Special Segment, U.C.L.A., 1986.

Post Graduate training through American Advertising Federation, 1990 - 1992.

Bachelor of Science, Advertising, University of Michigan, Flint, June 1984. Minor in Marketing

Consulting Experience

Consulted with Davis, Markham and Howard on corporate advertising campaign strategy for six major national corporate accounts. 1988 - 1991.

Independent consulting projects with three advertising agencies in Detroit area in the areas of market research, identifying market niche, product positioning, and new product development. 1987 - 1991.

Advertising Expertise

Worked as Advertising Manager for Simmons Machinery, Detroit, MI, 1987 - 1991.

Relevant course work in Advertising, Market Research, Consumer Behavior, Color Theory in Advertising, Business Statistics, Strategic Planning, Corporate Advertising and Public Relations.

Served as graduate instructor in Advertising at U.C.L.A. College of Business, 1984 - 1986.

Interpersonal Skills

Consistently received high performance appraisals from employees in anonymous evaluations at Simmons Machinery.

Known for ability to interact with small and large groups as well as individuals.

Elected student body president of University of Michigan for ability to represent a diversity of opinions and needs.

References

Provided on request

Yuji Uno
15 Front Avenue, N.W.
Washington, D.C. 20120
201/555-2988

OBJECTIVE   Seeking a position as Advertising Manager for a daily newspaper.

EXPERIENCE   **Capitol Weekly**
Washington, D.C.   9/90 to present
Advertising Sales Supervisor
Handle fifteen regular advertising accounts. Charged with developing client base. Developed sales strategies that posted net increases of 28% over the last two years. Increased regular advertiser inches by 18%. Work with design department to develop finished advertisements. Assist clients with concept development. Supervised staff of four sales representatives and support staff of two designers, two production artists, and three clerical workers. Work with Advertising Manager to determine sales projections and budgeting.

The Tennesseean
Nashville, TN   9/89 to 8/90
Advertising Sales
Handled twelve major accounts for statewide daily newspaper. Maintained advertising sales records for entire sales group. Developed in-house advertisements to promote display ads to potential clients. Made sales presentations. Developed and implemented reader survey and prepared analysis for use in demographic fact sheet to send to current and potential advertisers. Received Top Salesperson of the Month award for three consecutive months.

Nashville School District
Nashville, TN   2/78 to 8/89
Director of Public Information
Responsible for the direction and management of the school district's public information and community relations program. Assigned and wrote articles on activities, events, and programs pertaining to education. Took and developed photographs for inclusion in newsletters and news releases. Submitted weekly news releases to local media. Prepared all district publications to camera ready status in preparation for printing.

EDUCATION   **University of Tennessee,** Martin   1968 to 1972
Bachelor of Arts, Liberal Arts

University of Maryland, Baltimore County   1990 to 1992
Continuing Education: Advertising, Business Management, Business Operations, Consumer Behavior, Computer Applications in Business

REFERENCES   Available on request

JAMES ARTHUR KNOX
15829 Grant Avenue
Fargo, North Dakota 52289
(701) 555-9042

OBJECTIVE

Seeking a position as assistant traffic manager for a major advertising firm. Able to relocate anywhere in U.S.

EXPERIENCE

FARGO HERALD-TIMES   Sept. 1991 to present
Fargo, North Dakota
Production Manager
Responsible for the design of advertising supplements, classified and display advertisements using the Macintosh computer. Set deadlines and timelines for completing tasks associated with weekly newspaper.

SIR SPEEDY PRINT CENTER   Sept. 1989 to Aug. 1991
Bismarck, North Dakota
Graphic Artist/Typesetter
Performed varied duties as they relate to the printing industry. Primary areas of responsibility are typesetting on Macintosh IIcx with Linotronic 300 output, graphic design on Quark XPress and Adobe Illustrator, paste-up, stripping, and darkroom. Also involved in customer service and some outside sales. Handle all equipment maintenance and procurement.

INSTAGRAPHICS   Aug. 1986 to July 1988
Bismarck, North Dakota
Desktop Publishing Professional
Owned and operated small desktop publishing business. Made customer contact, developed marketing plan and materials, made presentations, prepared original designs based on client needs, and served as service bureau for other graphic designers. Hired staff of designers, production assistants, typesetters, and darkroom technicians. Coordinated with local print shop for quantity discounts.

EDUCATION

B.A. IN GRAPHIC DESIGN   Dec. 1985
Moore College of Art, Philadelphia, PA

A.A. IN PRINTING TECHNOLOGY   June 1981
North Dakota State University, Fargo, ND

ADDITIONAL COURSEWORK IN ADVERTISING   1990 & 1991
North Dakota State University, Fargo, ND

REFERENCES

Available upon request

Judith A. Washington

958 NW Sycamore, Amarillo, Texas 78077

Summary of Experience

806/555-0944

CAREER OBJECTIVES

To enhance advertising communications by utilizing computer graphics systems and/or traditional print media, and to work in a creative environment where my background in computers, graphics, and management will be used and further developed.

EXPERIENCE

Computer Graphics ■ Designed and produced drawings, charts, slides, video titles, large flip charts, newsletters, manuals, logos, ads, and brochures, using most major software programs on the Macintosh, IBM, and Amiga. Developed techniques and trained new employees in the use of computer graphics systems, evaluated and beta tested hardware and software.

Production Management ■ Coordinated and supervised employees and free-lancers in the creation of slides and manuals, and newspaper production. Hired and trained employees, maintained budgets, planned for fluctuating work loads and deadlines. Developed more efficient production procedures. Interacted with suppliers and clients. Met deadlines. Maintained hard disk storage and tape back-ups, typesetting and stat camera equipment, and ordered supplies. In traditional graphics, coordinated typesetting, photography, artwork, and printing on advertisements, brochures, newsletters, books, annual reports, catalogs, slides, and a newspaper.

Graphic Design ■ Translated concepts and information into appealing graphic text and images for advertisements, brochures, newsletters, charts, catalogs, packaging, newspaper ads, and video and slides. Skilled in type specification, creative layout, technical drawing, and spot illustration.

Typography ■ Created computer typefaces for a computer typography program. Excellent knowledge of typography. Experienced with various typesetting programs and traditional typesetting machinery.

Darkroom ■ Produced high quality stats, halftones, color keys, distortions, color separated negatives, and stripped film negatives.

JOB HISTORY

1988 – Present	Freelance: Presentation graphics, desktop publishing
1987 – 1988	Quality Printing Corporation, Palo Alto, CA
1985 – 1987	Prima Valley Publishing, Menlo Park, CA
1981 – 1985	Freelance: Graphic production and design
1979 – 1981	Graphic Productions, Menlo Park, CA
1976 – 1979	Flair Typographics, Itasca, IL
1975 – 1976	Art Packaging Corp., Des Plaines, IL
1973 – 1975	Kingsbury Corp., Des Plaines, IL

EDUCATION

1972, Associate Arts Degree, Graphic Design
American Academy of Art, Chicago, IL

1971, Bachelor of Arts Degree, Fine Art
Southern Illinois University, Carbondale, IL

References Available Upon Request

Lawrence P. Denning
P.O. Box 2286
Iowa City, IA 52244
319/555-0029

Objective:

Classified advertising sales and data entry position, swing shift.

Education:

Jefferson High School, Iowa City, IA
Expected graduation date, June 1993
Major: Journalism and Communications
Current G.P.A. 3.86

Planning to attend Iowa State University Journalism program.

Relevant Experience:

- Worked on student newspaper advertising staff, calling on potential
  and current advertisers to sell advertising space.
- Performed data entry of classified advertisements.
- Computed word count and rates for classified ads.
- Performed word processing functions.
- Assisted with layout and paste-up of newspaper.
- Took photographs with staff camera.

Activities & Achievements:

- Awarded First Place in Iowa High School Journalism Competition, Editorial
- Placed Second in Photography category, IHSJ Competition
- Worked as stage manager for student theatrical productions
- Honor Roll
- National Honor Society
- Member, Student Chapter, Iowa Newspaper Publishers Association

References

- Available on request

Ruth Solomon
330 Clarges Street, Apt. 24C
Salt Lake City, UT 83389
(801) 555-0938

Objective

To begin a career in advertising.

Education

Master of Arts in Journalism, The University of Iowa, Iowa City, May 1992
Area of Specialization: Advertising
GPA: 4.0

Courses:

Advertising Copywriting	Advertising Planning
Media Relations	Public Relations Writing
Corporate Communications	Consumer Behavior
Advertising Design	Production Technology

Bachelor of Science in Fisheries, University of Idaho, Moscow, June 1980

Relevant Experience

August 1990 - 1992	*Graduate Teaching Fellow, University of Iowa*
July 1980 - August 1990	*Fisheries Management/Information/Research* (details available on request for curriculum vitae)

Activities

Editor for International Association of Business Communicators, Utah Chapter.

Master's project on developing advertising, public service announcement, and mail campaign for the Alliance for Environmental Education.

Part-time proofreader of grant proposals and scientific reports, Iowa and Utah.

Member, International Association of Business Communicators, Society for Technical Communicators, and Phi Eta Kappa Advertising Honorary.

References

Available at University of Iowa Career Placement Center and on request.

JEANETTE SCHUMACHER
89 W. Morgan Avenue
Milwaukee, Wisconsin 53100
(419) 555-0824

JOB OBJECTIVE: **Permanent part-time work in the graphic arts and production department of a large advertising agency. Long-term goals: Complete a degree in advertising and design and obtain a full-time position in art direction.**

EDUCATION

Associate in Science Degree in Visual Communications
Milwaukee Community College, 1978. Curriculum included design and character generation, process camera, press work, typesetting, and black and white photography.

Currently enrolled in the undergraduate graphic design program with minor in advertising communications at the University of Wisconsin-Milwaukee.

EMPLOYMENT HISTORY

CAPITAL PRESS - **Newspaper (1986 to present)**
Broad Street & First, Milwaukee, WI
PASTE-UP ARTIST/TYPESETTER
Responsible for paste-up of newspaper pages, including classified and special advertising sections. Typeset and paste-up display advertisements and news copy. Also work in Creative Department as typesetter, where I prepare forms, newsletters, brochures, and other outside jobs. Equipment: Macintosh, Adwriter, MycroComp Newstouch, LaserWriter II, Linotronic 300, Compugraphic Integrator/PowerPage, 8400 laser printer, film processor, page proofer. Also maintain equipment and chemicals.

ADVANCED TYPOGRAPHICS - **Service Bureau (1983 - 1990)**
335 Lake Boulevard, Milwaukee, WI
TYPESETTER/PASTE-UP ARTIST
Typeset copy for magazines, newsletters, brochures, and advertisements. Paste-up of advertisements, newsletters, tabloid newspapers, and various other projects. Equipment: Compugraphic Integrator, 8400 laser printer, film processor.

MILWAUKEE GRAPHICS - **Graphic Design/Service Bureau (1984 - 1988)**
1156 Commercial Street, Milwaukee, WI
TYPESETTER/PASTE-UP ARTIST/PROCESS CAMERA OPERATOR
Responsibilities included setting type, working with clients to select type fonts and styles appropriate to the job, preparing paste-up of publications and books, and camera work (PMTs, PMT halftones, line shots). Equipment: Compugraphic 7500, stat camera.

REFERENCES AVAILABLE ON REQUEST

KARIN M. GILES
4019 West Hooper Road
Hagerstown, Maryland 03394
301/555-8476

EMPLOYMENT GOALS	Seeking an entry-level position in advertising, where I can put my organizational and financial skills to work and gain new knowledge and experience.
EDUCATION	Currently enrolled in advertising evening program at Central Community College. Relevant courses taken include advertising copywriting, business communications, marketing strategies, and ad sales planning.
WORK EXPERIENCE	MEDICAL OFFICE MANAGER, Henderson Chiropractic Clinic, Hagerstown, MD (October 1989 - current) Handled all insurance billing, accounts payable and receivable, payroll, daily ledger sheet balancing, patient billings, and medical report preparation. Supervised office staff, scheduled appointments, and worked effectively in a situation that required a significant amount of patient contact.
	ACCOUNTING CLERK, Riddle Press, Hagerstown, MD (March 1988 - September 1989) Managed full cycle bookkeeping, accounts payable and receivable, payroll, shift reports, switchboard operation. Completed computer data entry. Served as receptionist.
	BOOKKEEPER, Dr. Stephen L. Davis, Baltimore, MD (September 1984 - February 1987) Full cycle bookkeeping and office coordinator. Set up financial arrangements for orthodontic patients. Completed bi-monthly payroll. Processed statement and insurance billing and was responsible for collections. Scheduled appointments. Served as receptionist.
ADDITIONAL SKILLS	Over 12 years of office experience and customer relations. Typing approximately 65 wpm, 10-key, Covalent computer and printer data entry, multiline switchboard system. Have professional telephone techniques and work well with others.
REFERENCES	Furnished upon request.

Mary Elizabeth Bottaro
462 Main Street, Apt. 1
Durango, Colorado 81301
303/555-4546

Education

Fort Lewis College
Durango, CO
Advertising/Communications
Bachelor of Arts 1989

Career Experience

9/88 - 1/89
Rolling Stone Magazine
New York, NY
Research Intern
* Checked facts for publication
* Established positive rapport with professionals while preparing and confirming copy
* Organized and maintained research library
* Edited and proofread copy

8/85 - present
The Independent, FLC Newspaper
* **Awarded Writer of the Year** 1988
* **Writer** of political, editorial, social, hard news and features
* **Production Assistant** duties include layout and paste-up
* **Advertising Sales**
* Copyediting
* Typesetting

1/87 - 1/89
KRRK Channel 4/FLC News
* **Wrote, filmed, edited** weekly campus news cast

9/87 - 9/89
Passages, FLC Literary Arts Magazine
* **Editor** (1987-88)
* **Assistant Editor** (1988-89)
* Organized 12-member staff
* Obtained largest magazine budget in FLC history
* Established criteria and guidelines in selecting entries
* Maintained harmony with group decisions

Other Work Experience

Admissions assistant, Metropolitan Museum of Art, New York, NY
Library aide, Fort Lewis College Library, Durango, CO

Skills

* Photography (black and white, color)
* Macintosh Computer (graphics, page layout, word processing)
* NCR Computer (word processing, graphics)

Activities

* Scarlet Letters, FLC Communications Club
* Performed in FLC Theatre
* Volunteer at Burden Center for the Aging
* Concert Committee, FLC Student Government

References

Furnished on request

Carlos Diez

836 S. Marshall Street, Trenton, New Jersey 08776 / (609) 555-4310

Objective

Entry-level position as advertising copywriter with small to mid-sized agency.

Education

Newark College, Newark, NJ
B.A. in Communications with emphasis on Advertising, 1992

Accomplishments

- Worked as researcher in the advertising department of a major national magazine.
- Developed demographic profiles of magazine subscribers for advertiser information.
- Organized 12-member staff of advertising sales representatives for student newspaper.
- Oversaw all aspects of advertising department of student weekly newspaper.
- Determined and calculated ad space rates and frequency discounts.
- Wrote advertising copy for clients who lacked skilled staff writers.
- Worked with clients to develop advertising concepts.
- Produced a 10-ad series that won a regional advertising competition.
- Experienced in typesetting and copyediting for publication.
- Wrote news articles and feature stories for local media and student newspaper.
- Wrote, filmed, and edited weekly half-hour campus television news broadcast.
- Wrote, filmed, and edited television commercials for various student organizations.

Work History

- Advertising Manager, *The Newark News Week*, Newark College, Newark, NJ
- News Team, *WNC-TV*, Newark College, Newark, NJ
- Research Intern, Advertising Department, *Rolling Stone Magazine*, New York, NY

References

Available upon request.

SHARINA K. MYERS
5747 Pine Street SW
Shawnee, Oklahoma 74802
405/555-9371

OBJECTIVE: Seeking a position with the advertising department of a newspaper or magazine where my experience with writing, communications, and public relations may contribute to advertising sales as I gain new skills and begin reshaping my abilities for a new career.

EDUCATION

University of Oklahoma, Norman, OK: Master of Arts, Journalism (Advertising), 1992

University of Oklahoma, Norman, OK: Teacher Certification, English, 1983

Eastern New Mexico University, Portales, NM: Bachelor of Arts, English, 1976

Southwestern Oklahoma State University, Weatherford, OK: Bachelor of Arts, Journalism, 1974

PROFESSIONAL EXPERIENCE

The Quarter Horse Journal, Amarillo, TX: EDITORIAL COORDINATOR, January 1987-August 1990
Wrote short articles, assisted with editing, proofread all editorial and advertising copy, supervised copy flow between editorial and production departments, assisted with advertising sales.

Oklahoma Scoring Services, Norman, OK: ESSAY READER, January 1984-January 1987
Graded essays for the state GED examinations.

High School, Maysville, OK: TEACHER, August 1980 to June 1984
Taught English, Journalism, Speech. Served as yearbook adviser and newspaper adviser.

The Southwestern, Southwestern Oklahoma State University, Weatherford, OK: REPORTER, January-June 1974; ADVERTISING SALESPERSON, January-June 1973.
Assigned articles to student reporters, wrote and edited articles for the paper, chose copy to include in each issue, assisted in layouts and headline writing. Took calls for advertising department to reserve space for advertisements, developed advertising promotion ads and flyers to encourage sales of personal and business classified ads.

Public Relations Department, Southwestern Oklahoma State University: REPORTER, September 1972-May 1973.
Conducted interviews and wrote press releases on various faculty members and students at the college to be published in local newspapers and distributed to hometown newspapers.

REFERENCES ARE AVAILABLE ON REQUEST

Timony Blaisdell
P.O. Box 216B3
Boise, Idaho 83702
☎ 208.555.8920

Education

University of Idaho, Boise. Master of Arts. Major: Advertising. 1985. GPA 4.0.

Montana State University, Bozeman. Bachelor of Arts. Major: Journalism. 1977. GPA 3.87.

Professional Experience

Advertising Director, *The Boise Sun,* Boise, ID. August 1985 - present.
Responsibilities: Develop advertisements and promotions materials for advertising clients. Conduct periodic reader surveys and analyze responses with regard to demographics, marketing strategies, and subscription potential. Created ads that were directly responsible for producing $50,000 in additional advertising sales in a two-month period. Awarded two regional and one national American Newspaper Advertisers Association Honor Awards for in-house advertising design. Supervise staff of 6 advertising sales representatives and 5 graphic and production artists and typesetters.

Marketing Coordinator, Continuing Education Department, University of Idaho. 1980-1983.
Responsibilities: Plan and develop marketing strategy for attracting students to the university's Summer Term program. Write and design promotional literature, including bulletins, brochures, advertisements, and public service announcements. Coordinate with designers, typesetters, photographers, service bureaus, media advertising sales representatives and printers. Maintain advertising and promotion budget. Conduct surveys and evaluations.

Promotion Coordinator, InterArts Magazine, Boise, ID. 1977-1979.
Responsibilities: Coordinate all advertising sales for 12-page display advertising section in the back of the magazine, plus 2-page classified ad section. Make customer calls, develop ad rate cards and advertiser fact sheet, handle billing and collection. Schedule self-promotion advertising and exchange advertising with other publications. Maintain advertising budget.

News Editor, The Herald Independent, University of Boise student newspaper. 1975-1977.
Responsibilities: Write news copy, assign news stories to student reporters. Determine editorial content of newspaper hard-news pages. Coordinate feature stories with other staff editors. Assist with layout, copyediting, and production.

Honors

UI Graduate Teaching Fellowship, Journalism/Advertising, 1983-1985
UI Scholar's Award, 1985
MSU Scholarship and Leadership Award, 1975, 1976, 1977
MSU Dad's Club Scholarship, 1977
Millar Scholarship, 1973-1977
OES Scholarship, 1976
R.L. Underwood Scholarship, 1973-1977
Membership in University Honor Societies: Sigma Delta Chi and Kappa Tau Alpha (Journalism Honoraries), Phi Kappa Phi, Mortar Board, Alpha Lambda Delta, Talons, Phi Eta Sigma

References available on request

CHERYL SCOTT
1590 Junction Boulevard
Lexington, Kentucky 40506
606/555-7746

Position Objective: Advertising Copywriting

SKILLS & EXPERIENCE

Writing/Editing

- Developed, researched, and wrote general-audience guide book for outdoor recreation.
- Wrote copy for advertisements, brochures, flyers, and public service announcements.
- Widely published travel author, both magazines and newspapers.
- Developed advertising campaign and wrote copy for a series of 12 related ads.
- Wrote copy for mail order catalogs and book publishing/marketing catalogs.
- Wrote college-level textbook on public relations writing, including chapter on advertising writing.
- Taught college courses in advertising, public relations, and magazine writing.

Design/Production

- Designed and completed all aspects of production on several books.
- Served as co-publisher for small-press literary publishing house, producing 11 books.
- Designed and produced brochures and pamphlets in a variety of formats.
- Typeset and prepared camera-ready art for several books and brochures.
- Expert in desktop publishing and graphic design software.
- Designed advertisements and catalogs for various clients.

EDUCATION

University of Kentucky, School of Journalism.
- Master of Arts Degree, summa cum laude, 1989
- Emphasis, Advertising and Public Relations. Wrote graduate thesis on public relations writing, which was eventually published by Harcourt, Brace & Jovanovich.

Michigan State University, College of Liberal Arts.
- Bachelor of Arts Degree, with Highest Honors, 1979
- Major: English Literature

WORK EXPERIENCE

Advertising Coordinator, University of Kentucky, 1990-present.

Freelance Writer/Designer, various clients and publications, 1977-present.

Director of Communications, Michigan State University, 1979-1988.

References available upon request

BENJAMIN BLACKMORE
P.O. Box 5789
Sioux Falls, SD 57104
(605) 555-3758

CAREER OBJECTIVE

Seeking a position as advertising manager for a manufacturer.

EXPERIENCE

* Coordinated all aspects of high-level corporate visitations from prospective clients.

* Supervised corporate sales force of 128 sales representatives nationwide.

* Directed development of marketing strategies, new product development, and advertising and promotion planning.

* Delivered product presentations and demonstrations.

* Designed and wrote product marketing guides, competitive reports, and training materials for field representatives.

* Responsible for software installation, applications support, troubleshooting, and maintenance for 25 accounts.

* Presented sales demonstrations and provided training and customer service for installed accounts.

* Assisted with sales office activities.

WORK HISTORY

Hutchison Computer Corporation, Sioux Falls, SD, 1984 - present
* Senior Sales Support Analyst, 1989 - present
* Field Marketing Specialist, 1986 - 1989
* System Analyst, 1984 - 1986

Market Systems Corporation, Rapid City, SD, 1976 - 1983
* Customer Support Manager
* Support Analyst

Blackmore & Gwynne, Inc., Minneapolis, MN, 1972 - 1976
* Educational Services Representative
* Sales and Marketing Representative

EDUCATION

University of Minnesota, Minneapolis-St. Paul
* B.S. in Business Administration, 1972
* Minor: Advertising and Marketing

REFERENCES AVAILABLE

Edward G. McDonald
23 Battersea Street
Portland, Maine 04129
(207) 555-9365

Objective

A position as an advertising account executive with a firm handling primary products and manufacturing accounts.

Experience

- Managed 34 national accounts for the timber, agriculture, and steel industries.

- Worked with advertising sales representatives from print and broadcast media to negotiate space rates for clients.

- Headed creative teams charged with developing corporate identity, advertising campaign strategies, and sponsorship promotions.

- Designed and directed development of several advertising campaigns, two of which won national awards for both concept and net result.

- Experienced with analysis of demographic data and market survey reports.

- Created and implemented coordinated advertising, direct mail, and promotional campaigns.

- Initiated all advertising and sales promotional materials for U.S. Steel.

- Served as media buyer for a major New York advertising agency.

Work History

Haddon, Briden, and Walsh, Portland, ME. Associate Account Executive. 1990-present

Bacher Spielvogel Bates, Inc., New York. Advertising Account Assistant. 1983-1990

BBDO Worldwide Inc., New York. Media Buyer, 1977-1982

Roy Ross Group, Inc., Bloomfield Hills, MI. Advertising Assistant. 1975-1977

Education

Michigan State University, East Lansing, MI. BA in Business Administration, 1975.
Emphasis: Advertising and Corporate Communications

References

Available on request

Jerome Marcus
2235 E. 27th Street
Bronx, NY 10009
212/555-2875

Objective: A position as advertising assistant where I can use my planning, marketing, and design skills.

Skills & Experience:

Handled four accounts for advertising agency.

Wrote copy, designed, and laid out advertisements.

Assisted with traffic control.

Served as liaison between clients and account executives.

Assisted in designing ads for magazine publication.

Computed ad sizes and rates.

Translated data from dummy production worksheets for distribution and review.

Assisted with market research survey development.

Implemented developments in advertising rate card and informational packet that directly contributed to increased advertising sales.

Work History

Advertising Intern, Bozell, Inc., New York, NY. Summer 1992

Advertising Assistant, part-time, Manhattan Digest Magazine, New York, NY. 1989-1992

Classified Advertising Sales, New York Daily News, Long Island, NY. 1988-1989

Education

Collegiate High School of the Bronx, 1992 graduate
Major: Business and Advertising
GPA: 3.86 in major courses, 3.4 overall

Activities

President, Business Club
Vice President, Student Marketing Association
Treasurer, National Honor Society
Student Representative, Bronx District School Board
Volunteer, Central Bronx Hospice

References available

Trent Garrison
335 La Paluma Blvd.
San Francisco, California 94163
415/555-3968

Objective

Video production specialist and animator for large advertising production company.

Skills and Accomplishments

Won Oscar nomination for special effects productions in major motion picture.

Won Graphic Arts Best in Category Award for computer-generated animation series.

Won California Animation Society Award for computer-generated advertisement.

Produced more than 50 highly sophisticated animated advertisements for a wide variety of corporate and industrial clients.

Designed and produced trademark and logo animation sequences for film corporations and television stations.

Assisted in creative design teams for special effects production in 17 major motion pictures.

Headed creative team for special effects production on 2 films.

Maintained budget for design and production staff of small video production company.

Employment History

Industrial Light & Magic, San Jose, CA. 1984 - 1992
• Creative Team Leader, 1990 - 1992
• Design and Animation Production, 1986 - 1990
• Production Technician, 1984 - 1986

VideoGraphics, San Francisco, CA. 1978 - 1984
• Production Department Manager, 1981 - 1984
• Animator, 1978 - 1980

Education

Pratt Institute, Brooklyn, NY
MFA, Video Arts and Computer Graphics, 1978

San Francisco Art Institute, CA
BFA, Graphic Design, 1976

References available as requested

Marnie Valentine
427 Savannah Avenue
Savannah, Georgia 30292
(912) 555-9775

Experience

Assisted sales staff of advertising agency in areas of research and demographics.

Prepared sales forecasts from available data.

Identified potential target markets for new products.

Worked with creative team to develop ad concepts and marketing strategies.

Researched and compiled sales reports on consumer behavior patterns for a wide variety of products and services.

Made professional presentation of advertising campaign proposals.

Directed student advertising studio.

Arranged filing and reporting systems on computer hardware.

Organized department inventory.

Work History

Advertising Studio, Director, University of Georgia, Athens, GA, 1991-92.

Advertising Intern, Waite and Rand Associates, Savannah, GA, Summer 1992.

Research Intern, Waite and Rand Associates, Savannah, GA, Summer 1991.

Education

University of Georgia, Athens, GA
Bachelor of Science degree in Advertising, 1992

Honors

Superior Service Award, Waite and Rand Associates, 1992
American Advertising Federation Merit Award, Collegiate Regional Competition, 1991
Dean's List

References

On file with Career Center, University of Georgia, Athens, and on request

Juanita Rodriguez-Sutton
330 Hollywood Boulevard
Los Angeles, California   90063
(213) 555-2475 days
(213) 555-0248 message

Career Objective: Seeking opportunity to put my marketing background and skills to work for a progressive advertising agency.

Experience

ૐ Handled distribution, retail marketing, advertising, and mail order marketing.
ૐ Wrote advertising copy and distributed to clients and account executives.
ૐ Obtained knowledge of domestic and overseas regulations for trademarks.
ૐ Assisted marketing director with radio and television promotion and retail marketing.
ૐ Coordinated radio and print interview opportunities for visiting artists and writers.
ૐ Developed and implemented marketing plans for major retail chain.
ૐ Directed research department for market data and sales reports.

Work History

LA Productions Weekly, Los Angeles, CA
ૐ Marketing Director, 9/88 to present
ૐ Public Relations/Marketing Assistant, 6/82 to 7/88

KBOO Radio, Venice, CA
ૐ Marketing and Promotions Director, 5/77 to 6/80
ૐ Promotions Assistant, 3/76 to 5/77

Education

University of California, Los Angeles
ૐ Post baccalaureate study in Advertising and Marketing, 9/80 to 6/82
ૐ Bachelor of Science in Journalism/Public Relations, 6/76

References are available upon request

QUENTIN SANTORINI
4325 Whitehall
Burlington, VT 05401
802-555-9876

JOB OBJECTIVE

A challenging entry-level position as a graphic artist in an advertising department or agency.

EXPERIENCE

Produced line drawings to illustrate magazine articles.

Prepared computer graphics images for slide presentations.

Developed promotional materials, including advertisements and brochures.

Handled all aspects of production, from layout to finished product, for university publications office.

Completed storyboards for television commercial series.

Took photographs for publication in student newspaper.

Assisted in page layout on computer.

EDUCATION

University of Vermont, Burlington, VT
B.A. in Illustration, May 1992

WORK HISTORY

Vermont Harvester Magazine, Burlington, VT
Commercial Artist, Summers 1989 - 1992

University of Vermont, Burlington, VT
Designer, University Publications Department, 1989 - 1992

Photographer/Production Assistant, Student Newspaper, 1990 - 1992

WORKSHOPS

Desktop Publishing with Microsoft Word, 1992
Graphic Arts on the Desktop, 1992
New England Design Seminar, 1991

References are available on request

Selina   Morales

Present Address   Permanent Address
234 Lynn Rock Road   288 Monroe Drive
Kansas City, MO 64121   Excelsior Springs, MO 64024
816/555-0567

Objective: Advertising copywriting.

Education:

University of Missouri, Kansas City
Expected date of graduation, December, 1992. Degree:
Bachelor of Arts in advertising with a minor in
marketing.

Work   Experience:

Weekly Sentinel, Kansas City, MO (part-time, August 1991
to present)
Responsibilities include ad sales, ad copywriting, order-
handling, customer relations, data entry, proofreading.
Distribute checking copy to department heads.

The Kansas Advertiser, Kansas City, MO (full-time, June
1991 to September 1991)
Special studies intern: responsibilities included design
and layout of display advertisements, classified ad
sales, and ad copywriting.

Related   Coursework:

Advertising Copywriting, Advertising Design, Advertising
Campaigns, Public Relations Writing and Research,
Electronic Design and Production, Business
Communications, News Writing

Activities:

Sigma Delta Chi journalism honorary, Advertising Club,
Kansan (university student yearbook) advertising sales
and copyeditor, Pi Beta Phi national sorority

References and portfolio available on request.

P. Marilyn Pederson   2274 Acorn Place • Santa Fe, New Mexico 87538
                                                              505.555.2176

CAREER OBJECTIVE

Seeking a challenging position as Art Director with a Santa Fe advertising agency.

EXPERIENCE

- Responsible for overseeing all projects in small advertising/typesetting studio.
- Handle all daily business.
- Supervise three typesetters and four artist/designers.
- Completed projects include: print media space advertisements, catalogs, P.O.P., direct mail, consumer, business to business and recruitment advertising with a wide variety of accounts.
- Managed three-person art department.
- Supervised layout, design, illustration, and production of consumer, recruitment, and automotive accounts.
- Production of layout, design, illustration, storyboards, and production for corporate headquarters, financial, insurance, and travel sections.
- Handled overload from JC Penney store advertising department.
- As freelance designer, provided advertisement design, layout, and production for wide range of clients, including newspaper advertising department, automotive dealership, financial organizations, and advertising agencies.

WORK HISTORY

Creative Advertising Designs, Inc./Santa Fe   1988 to present
Senior Designer, Production Manager, Account Executive.

Patterson & Associates, Marketing & Advertising Agency/Santa Fe   1986-1988
Designer, Production Manager

JC Penney Corporation, Corporate Advertising Department/New York   1981-1986
Senior Artist, Staff Artist, Production Assistant

Freelance Designer/New York   1980-1988

EDUCATION & SEMINARS

San Francisco Art Institute/California
Bachelor of Fine Arts Degree, Graphic Design & Illustration, 1980

How to Choose a Service Bureau/New York
Two-week seminar on printing specifications, purchasing, and related services, 1984

MEMBERSHIPS

Graphic Design Association/Santa Fe
American Association of Graphic Artists/National

REFERENCES are available upon request.

SHAWN RIVENER
2660 N. Grand
Billings, Montana 59105
406.555.5373 (days)
406.555.3954 (eves)

CAREER OBJECTIVE

Seeking an assistant art director's position with an advertising agency that will utilize my skills in computer graphics and desktop publishing.

TECHNICAL SKILLS

- design
- illustration
- typesetting
- display advertisements
- logos
- forms

- layout
- copywriting
- magazines
- flyers
- letterheads
- reports

- production art
- editing
- newsletters
- posters
- business cards
- graphs

EQUIPMENT/SOFTWARE EXPERIENCE

- Compugraphic Editwriter
- WordPerfect
- Quark XPress
- MacPaint

- AM Varityper equipment
- PageMaker
- Aldus Freehand
- Corel Draw

- IBM and Macintosh
- Microsoft Word
- Adobe Illustrator
- Harvard Graphics

EMPLOYMENT HISTORY

Graphic Plus, Billings, Montana. February 1986 - present
Chief designer, editor, typesetter
- Prepare posters, design event-specific logos.
- Produce brochures and other mailing pieces.
- Handle all typesetting, design, production functions for small design agency.

A & S Typesetting, Billings, Montana. November 1981 - January 1986
Production artist, typesetter
- Responsible for typesetting, layout, paste-up.
- Served as copywriter and ad artist for tabloid and magazine clients.

Billings Printing Center, Billings, Montana, June 1977 - November 1981
Production artist
- Provided clients with typesetting and clip art produced advertising, newsletters, brochures, flyers, tabloids, and other products.

EDUCATION

Montana Community College, Billings, Montana
Awarded two Associates degrees in Printing Production (1977) and Graphic Design (1986)

References available upon request

Mariah Udey

11240 Paradise Way • Las Vegas, Nevada 89102 • (702) 555-2485

JOB OBJECTIVE

To obtain a position on a creative team with an advertising agency that will challenge my background and skills in design, account representation, and strategic planning.

PROFESSIONAL EXPERIENCE

Swenson, Greves, and Huber, Inc., Las Vegas   March 1980 - Present
Senior Designer, Assistant Account Executive

- Hold complete responsibility for four major accounts which I brought to the agency.
- Participate on creative team for six major accounts.
- Participate in corporate strategic planning.
- Plan and balance client needs, goals, and budget considerations.
- Direct staff and work with freelancers.
- Provide press approvals and direct activity of graphic department.
- Make recommendations to clients for campaign strategies, concepts, and development.

Harrah's Club, Las Vegas   June 1972 - February 1977
Advertising Department Manager

- Planned and designed national advertising campaigns for major hotel and casino operation.
- Worked extensively with television and radio production agency to develop broadcast ads.
- Assisted with national advertising campaigns for major entertainment facility.
- Designed and directed graphic artists in preparation of advertisements.

EDUCATION

University of Nevada, Las Vegas
Master's Degree in Business Administration, 1980
Dual Bachelor's Degrees in Graphic Design and Advertising, 1979
Associates Degree in Design and Illustration, 1972

References available

TOBY MORRISON
3352 W. Evans Drive
Suncook, New Hampshire 03725
(603) 555-4876

EXPERIENCE

- Designed and developed product display concepts.

- Illustrated renderings

- Coordinated computer graphic design orders for client jobs

- Held responsible for inventory control and product distribution.

- Developed concepts and carried them to camera ready state, production, or actual print.

- Examples of graphic works include book covers, program layout.

- Established clientele and maintained customer service.

- Responsible for scheduling, security, customer service, and payroll.

WORK HISTORY

DESIGN ENGINEER, Darvol Corporation, Concord, NH	May 1991 - present
DESIGNER, Self-employed	June 1988 - present
SUPPORT STAFF, Traver Gallery, Concord, NH	March 1990 - May 1991
MANAGER, Concord Bar and Grill, Concord, NH	May 1989 - March 1990

EDUCATION

Bachelor of Arts, Arts Administration, University of New Hampshire	May 1989

AFFILIATIONS

Progressive Design Group of New Hampshire
Alpha Lambda, Arts Honorary

SPECIAL SKILLS

Apple Macintosh design applications:
Aldus PageMaker
Adobe Illustrator
Apple Scan
Claris CAD
Mac Draw
Quark XPress
Ultra Paint
Virtus Walkthrough
Also familiar with general office applications and similar IBM applications.

REFERENCES AND PORTFOLIO AVAILABLE UPON REQUEST

Penny Miller Harrison
1644 Craft Lane
Jersey City, New Jersey 07306
201/555-1197

OBJECTIVE: *To join the advertising department of a large organization where my skills in marketing may be directed toward advertising.*

EDUCATION: *Master of Arts, Business Administration,* December 1992
Stanford University, Stanford, California
G.P.A. 3.8
Relevant Courses:

Business Administration	Organizational Dynamics
Marketing	Advertising Management
Advertising Copywriting	Financial Management
Policy and Procedures Planning	Legal Issues in Advertising
Research Methods	

Bachelor of Science, Design, May 1987
University of Pennsylvania, Philadelphia
G.P.A. 3.6
Relevant Courses:

Graphic Design	Logo and Trademark Design
Advertising Design	Graphic Design Production
Typography	Packaging Design

EXPERIENCE:

1987-1990 *New Jersey State Arts Foundation*
Program Assistant
Designed flyers, posters, and advertisements announcing competitions. Served as administrative assistant to public art program coordinator. Researched other public art programs for policy development purposes. Prepared detailed reports on the program's operational effectiveness. Systematized slide registry and project files. Assisted in art and artist selection procedures. Coordinated selection committee meetings and slide presentations. Served as communication link between director, artists, and committees.

1985-1987 *Composition Experts, Inc., Philadelphia, PA*
Laser Printer Operator
Served as operator of computer source laser printers. Designed logos and forms using IBM/Xerox/Intran combination. Produced and distributed laser print and microfiche. Some programming and troubleshooting of laser printers.

HONORS:

Summa cum laude, Stanford University
Phi Beta Kappa
Dean's Honors
Stanford Business Fellowship
Senior Design Scholarship Award, University of Pennsylvania
Member of several scholarship honorary societies

REFERENCES: Provided upon request.

Helena W. Greenlea
323 North Fountain Drive
Baltimore, MD 21225
301/555-8846

Objective: Advertising Director for major publishing firm.

Recent Experience:

Advertising Consultant, Berriman and Associates, Baltimore, MD. 1985 to present
Managing Director, advertising consulting firm for advertising departments of magazine and
newspaper publishers, manufacturers, distributors, and entrepreneurs.

Management	Direct staff of creative advertising campaign managers, graphic artists, and advertising sales experts in providing consulting services to nationwide clients. Handle all budget, payroll, personnel, and management concerns.
Creative Solutions	Conceptualize management solutions for advertising departments of publishing firms, dealing with team strategy development, account management, and organization restructuring.
Marketing Strategies	Produce advertising campaign plans translating clients' information into concrete form and scheduling. Work closely with clients to help identify product markets, target advertising messages, and appropriate media delivery.
Art Direction	Direct creative work for print and film advertisements, brochure literature, books, publications, catalogs, posters, logos, trademarks, annual reports, labels and packages, slide programs, animated sequences, and games.

Advertising Manager, Holt, Rinehart & Winston, New York, NY. 1965 to 1985
Twenty years of experience with all aspects of advertising for the nation's third largest book
publisher. Also experienced with magazine division advertising programs, including
advertising space sales.

Education: Bachelor of Science, Business Administration, 1964
Minor: Advertising and Marketing Promotions
Westminster College, New Wilmington, PA

References furnished on request

Francine Masters
222 Market Street, N.W.
San Francisco, CA 94108
(415) 555-1223

Goal	To obtain a position as an assistant advertising account executive.

Work Experience

Advertising Coordinator, 1990-present
501 Union Center, San Francisco

- Coordinate media planning and buying for 20-store shopping center
- Research potential markets for ad campaigns
- Supervise artwork, layout, and production
- Handle sales promotions

Assistant Coordinator of Advertising, 1985-1989
Macy's, San Francisco, California

- Supervised trade shows and press shows
- Arranged and conducted sales meetings and presentations
- Designed and distributed press packets
- Developed marketing strategies
- Planned marketing and advertising campaigns
- Wrote and distributed press releases
- Served as liaison between clients and media representatives
- Acted as liaison to outside advertising agencies

Assistant Sales Manager, 1983-1984
Macy's, San Francisco

Salesperson, 1982-1983
Macy's, San Francisco

Education

Bachelor of Arts, Philosophy, 1981
Wesleyan University, Middletown, Connecticut

Honors

Junior Women's Scholarship
Dean's List
Senior Essay Award, Philosophy

References

Available on request.

Winston W. Brussard, Jr.
212 N. Jefferson Street
Albany, Georgia 31701
912-555-2239

Objective   An ad sales position leading to a career in advertising management.

Sales Experience

Served as salesperson in sporting goods store. Over six-month period, made consistent increases in sales, which led to my being selected as salesperson of the quarter, spring 1992.

Worked with advertising sales staff of student publications, both newspaper and yearbook. Made calls on local businesses, determined advertisement rates, and assisted with billing and bookkeeping.

Leadership

Elected Senior Class Vice President, 1991-92. Responsible for overseeing committees, served as senior class representative to Student Senate. Assumed responsibilities of class President in her absence.

Revived Business Club; served as President, 1991-92. Set meeting agendas, presided over meetings, instituted fund drive to sponsor professional visitations and field trips, organized trips to local business organizations.

Management

Managed Student Store, Monroe High School, 1991-92. Supervised student clerks, scheduled work shifts, ordered supplies, received shipments and checked them against purchase orders, served customers.

Served as Weekend Night Manager at a 125-room motel. Greeted guests, managed registration desk, supervised night staff, and served as security representative on alternating weekends.

Work History

Weekend Night Manager, Motel Orleans, Albany, GA, July 1992 - present
Salesperson, Jefferson's Sporting Goods, Albany, GA, May 1991 - June 1992
Advertising Sales, Monroe High School Student Publications, Albany, GA. June 1989 - May 1991

Education

Monroe High School, Albany, Georgia
Graduation class of 1993

Activities & Memberships: Business Club, Newspaper, Yearbook, Forensics Club, National Honor Society, Pep Club, Publicity Committee, Photography Club, JV and Varsity Wrestling

References   Available on request

§ STEWART SULLIVAN §

OBJECTIVE   To secure a position on the production staff of an advertising agency where I may utilize my skills with graphic design, typesetting, and layout.

EXPERIENCE   Graphic Artist, Student Yearbook Staff, 1990-92

§ Assumed responsibility for overall design concepts in 212-page hardbound yearbook.

§ Provided design assistance to editorial staff. Developed graphic elements for pages needing art work.

§ Designed page layouts and prepared camera-ready mechanicals for all advertising pages.

§ First year, used all traditional layout and paste-up methods. Second year, incorporated computer page-layout technology with desktop publishing software.

§ Prepared photographs for publication (cropped, sized).

§ Supervised staff of production assistants.

Production Assistant, Borah Gazette, 1989-91

§ Prepared paste-up boards for student newspaper.

§ Used light table to crop halftones.

§ Designed graphics for accenting advertisement section.

Typesetter, Borah Gazette, 1989-90

§ Input copy and headlines on Compugraphic 2420, using appropriate codes for setting line length, type fonts, styles, and sizes.

EDUCATION   Borah Senior High School, Boise, Idaho
Class of 1993. Grade point average in art: 4.0.

Areas of study: Journalism, Photojournalism, Graphic Design, Art (painting, drawing, watercolor, ceramics)

REFERENCES   Available on request.

1220 North Cole Road   §   Boise, Idaho 83709   §   208/555-2477

Jasmine Kiloiku ❖ 4223 Kilauea Avenue ❖ Honolulu, Hawaii 96819 ❖ 808/555-4378

Objective   ❖ Account Assistant with small to mid-sized advertising agency.

Experience   ❖ Benton Simmons Matea & Foley, Inc., Honolulu, HI
1988 to present
Display Advertising Media Buyer

Technical knowledge of advertising, design, pre-press, and printing
functions. Experienced in budgeting, pricing strategies, and proposal
writing. Coordinate all local advertising for seven major corporate
clients. Through market analysis, identified prime media outlets and pursued
advantageous advertising contracts for several clients.

❖ Kaui Container Corporation, Honolulu, HI
1986 to 1988
Marketing and Promotion Coordinator

Organized and produced special events. Prepared all advertising and
promotion materials. Produced quarterly design awards program.
Participated in development of Kaui sales literature. Designed sales
presentations using computer graphics presentation software on Macintosh.
Planned and implemented effective advertising, public relations, and dealer
incentive programs.

Education   ❖ Bachelor of Arts, Liberal Studies, 1985
Hawaii Pacific College, Honolulu, HI

References   ❖ Furnished as requested

CAMERON D. FLYNN

2820 West Braddock Road
Alexandria, Virginia 22302
Telephone: 703.555-4761

EMPLOYMENT OBJECTIVE

Advertising Account Executive with a growing, progressive advertising agency.

EMPLOYMENT EXPERIENCE

Virginia State Bank, Alexandria
Marketing/Advertising Director, 1989 - present

* Research target markets and competitive markets.
* Prepared complete marketing plan for introducing new line of banking services.
* Negotiated media space purchases in local news media.
* Coordinated production of television and radio commercials with contract production agency.
* Designed art work and coordinated production for posters, flyers, brochures, and advertisements.
* Designed and prepared all in-house informational materials.

Alexandria Water and Electric Board
Advertising Coordinator, 1987 - 1989

* Prepared advertising plans for all changes in operations procedures or rates.
* Purchased advertising space in local print media.
* Designed and produced advertisements for publications.
* Coordinated production of quarterly 24-page newsletter to consumers.
* Sold advertising space in newsletter.

AccuPartners, Inc.
Computer Support Specialist, 1982 - 1985

* Provided instruction for clients in the use of accounting software.
* Provided basic accounting instruction and training in the preparation of income statements and balance sheets.
* Prepared reports with line specifications and custom features.
* Provided additional support for all software users.

Brentwood, Stevens and Associates, Inc.
Accountant, 1978 - 1982

* Collected data and prepared weekly, monthly, and yearly reports.
* Prepared cost and profit reports, generated revision reports.
* Communicated with banks and other financial institutions.

ACADEMIC BACKGROUND

Virginia Academy of Business
Associate Degree in Advertising, 1987

Alexandria Community College
Associate Degree in Accounting, 1977

REFERENCES are available upon request.

VIRGINIA CONSTABLE
2248 Willow Road, Apt. 23
Louisville, KY 40215-7682
502/555-8475

JOB OBJECTIVE

To manage a creative advertising program for a small but growing computer technology firm.

EXPERIENCE

Self-Employed Creative Director, Louisville, KY
January 1988 to present
• Created an advertising and publications service company.
• Responsible for new business development.
• Managed seven statewide advertising accounts.
• Published a bi-monthly 28-page full-color magazine for one client. Provided all copywriting, design, and production services as well as advertising sales and self-promotion ads.
• Assisted on production and advertising development for local business newspaper.
• Advertising development, sales, and production account for approximately 40% of activity.

Director of Advertising, Westport International, Louisville, KY
November 1983 to March 1988
• Coordinated all national and regional advertising efforts for this international clothing retailer.
• Supervised all creative development and broadcast production through a contract agency.
• Developed all collateral print production.
• Supervised regional media buying for 58-store co-operative.
• Responsible for local store marketing efforts for 36 Midwest franchise-operated stores.
• Created all corporate self-promotion materials.
• Developed community ties through sponsorships of local organizations.
• Trained all new franchise owners and store managers on in-store marketing and advertising.

Media Buyer, Westport International, Louisville, KY
September 1980 to November 1983
• Served as media buyer for company-owned outlets in Kentucky.
• Television and radio buyer for the Midwest Regional Marketing Association co-op.
• Conducted regional and national image and awareness survey.
• Developed, produced, and implemented an in-store customer response survey.
• Evaluated all company store sales results from target advertising campaigns.

EDUCATION

University of Kentucky
Bachelor of Arts, Business and Management, 1979
Minor: Communications/Advertising

ACTIVITIES

Board of Directors, Mid-Kentucky Advertising Association
Speaker, University of Kentucky Career Fair
Woodie Award Recipient, Excellence and Achievement Award, seven awards from 1985 to 1991
American Advertising Federation member since 1980

References will be furnished on request.

JAMES MARCHINGTON
15829 First Avenue
Battle Creek, MI 49017
(616) 555-9042

OBJECTIVE

Seeking a position as assistant production manager for a Chicago-area advertising firm.

EXPERIENCE

BATTLE CREEK REPORTER   Sept. 1991 to present
Battle Creek, MI
Production Manager
• Responsible for the design of advertising supplements, classified and display advertisements.
• Experienced with page layout on the Macintosh computer.
• Set deadlines and timelines for completing tasks associated with weekly newspaper.
• Supervise crew of production artists, photographers, and designers to assure timely, quality production.

MICHIGAN PRINT CENTER   Sept. 1989 to Aug. 1991
Battle Creek, MI
Graphic Artist/Typesetter
• Performed varied tasks related to the printing industry.
• Primary areas of responsibility are typesetting on Macintosh IIcx with Linotronic 300 output.
• Produced page layout and graphic design on Quark XPress and Adobe Illustrator.
• Assisted with paste-up, stripping, and darkroom preparation.
• Involved in customer service and some outside sales.
• Handled all equipment maintenance and procurement.

GRAPHICS PLUS   Aug. 1986 to July 1988
Detroit, MI
Desktop Publishing Assistant
• Worked for small desktop publishing business.
• Made customer contact, developed marketing plan and materials.
• Made presentations and prepared original designs based on client needs.
• Output products prepared by other graphic designers.

EDUCATION

A.A. IN GRAPHIC PRODUCTION TECHNIQUES   Dec. 1985
Sanders College of Art, Detroit, MI

A.A. IN PRINTING TECHNOLOGY   June 1981
Michigan State University, Battle Creek, MI

ADDITIONAL COURSEWORK IN ADVERTISING   1990 & 1991
Michigan State University, Battle Creek, MI

REFERENCES

Available upon request

MICHELLE A. SUTTER
P.O. Box 18
ANN ARBOR, MI 48106
(313) 555-3758

OBJECTIVE

Seeking a position as advertising market analyst.

EXPERIENCE

Hutchison Computer Corporation, Ann Arbor, MI, 1984 - present
* Senior Sales Support Analyst, 1989 - present
* Field Marketing Specialist, 1986 - 1989
* System Analyst, 1984 - 1986

  Directed development of marketing strategies, new product
  development, and advertising and promotion planning.
  Coordinated all aspects of high-level corporate visitors for
  prospective customers requiring site participation by
  management and marketing division directors. Supervised
  corporate sales force of 128 sales representatives
  nationwide.

Intel Systems Corporation, Rapid City, SD, 1976 - 1983
* Customer Support Manager
* Support Analyst

  Delivered product presentations and demonstrations. Designed
  and wrote product marketing guides, competitive reports, and
  training materials for field sales and service
  representatives. Responsible for software installation,
  applications support, troubleshooting, and maintenance for 25
  accounts.

Computer Technology Associates, Madison, WI, 1972 - 1976
* Educational Services Representative
* Sales and Marketing Representative

  Presented sales demonstrations and negotiated equipment
  sales. Provided training and customer service for installed
  accounts. Assisted with sales office activities.

EDUCATION

University of Wisconsin, Madison
* B.S. in Business Administration, 1972
* Minor: Advertising and Marketing

REFERENCES AVAILABLE

Sander Feldstein

Objective

A position as advertising account executive in the Raleigh, North Carolina, area.

Experience

Haddon, Briden, and Walsh, Portland, ME. Associate Account Executive.
  1990-present

- Managed 34 national accounts for the agriculture, packaging and garment industries.

- Worked with advertising sales representatives from print and broadcast media to negotiate space rates for clients.

- Headed creative teams charged with developing corporate identity, advertising campaign strategies, and sponsorship promotions.

Bacher Spielvogel Bates, Inc., New York. Advertising Account Assistant.
  1983-1990

- Designed and directed development of several advertising campaigns, two of which won national awards for both concept and net result.

- Experienced with analysis of demographic data and market survey reports.

- Created and implemented cooperative advertising, direct mail, and promotional campaigns.

BBDO Worldwide Inc., New York. Media Buyer.
  1977-1982

- Initiated all advertising and sales promotional materials for U.S. Steel.

- Served as media buyer for major New York advertising agency.

Roy Ross Group, Inc., Bloomfield Hills, MI. Advertising Assistant.
  1975-1977

- Provided analysis of demographic data and developed market survey reports.

- Assisted with advertising, direct mail, and promotional campaigns for wide range of clients.

Education

Michigan State University, East Lansing, MI. BA in Business Administration, 1975.
Emphasis: Advertising and Corporate Communications

References available on request

283 Silver Street•Durham, North Carolina 27701•(919) 555-9365

Tawana Mitchell
427 Portland Avenue, No. 22
Bridgewater, MA 02324
(508) 362-9775

Job Sought   Entry-level position in the field of advertising account management.

Experience

Advertising Studio, Director, University of Chicago, Chicago, IL, 1991-92.

Directed student advertising studio. Worked with creative team to develop ad concepts and marketing strategies. Made professional presentation of advertising campaign proposals. Organized department inventory.

Advertising Intern, Faulk & Strand Associates, Chicago, IL, Summer 1992.

Assisted sales staff of advertising agency in areas of research and demographics. Prepared sales forecasts from available data. Identified and researched potential target markets for new products.

Research Intern, Faulk & Strand Associates, Chicago, IL, Summer 1991.

Researched and compiled sales reports on consumer behavior patterns for a wide variety of products and services. Arranged filing and reporting systems on computer hardware.

Education

University of Chicago, Chicago, Illinois
Bachelor of Science degree in Advertising, 1992

Honors & Activities

Superior Service Award, Faulk & Strand Associates, 1992
American Advertising College Honor Award, Collegiate National Competition, 1991
Dean's List
President, Student Council on Equality
Appointed to the Chancellor's Committee for the Status of Women
Served on University of Chicago Advertising Department Faculty Search Committee

References

On file with Placement Board Office, University of Chicago, and on request.

Stephen Tyrol

330 Copley Road ◆ Akron, Ohio 44308 ◆ (216) 555-2475 ◆ (216) 555-0248 (msg)

Objective: A career in advertising account management.

Related Career Experience

MidWest Clothiers, Akron, OH
◆ Marketing Assistant Director, 9/88 to present
◆ Public Relations/Marketing Assistant, 6/82 to 9/88

   ◇ Handled distribution, retail marketing, advertising, and mail order marketing.
   ◇ Wrote advertising copy and distributed to advertising executives.
   ◇ Obtained knowledge of domestic and overseas regulations for trademarks.
   ◇ Developed and implemented marketing plans for major retail chain.

WIJO TV/WGMA FM Radio, Boston, MA
◆ Marketing and Promotions Assistant, 5/77 to 6/80
◆ Research Assistant, 3/76 to 5/77

   ◇ Assisted marketing director with radio and television promotion and retail marketing.
   ◇ Coordinated radio and print interview opportunities for visiting artists and writers.
   ◇ Directed research department for market data and sales reports.

Education

University of Massachusetts, Amherst
◆ Post baccalaureate study in Advertising and Marketing, 9/80 to 6/82
◆ Bachelor of Science in Journalism/Public Relations, 6/76

References are available upon request

WENDY MILLER

PRESENT ADDRESS
122 Ketchum Hwy
Auburn, Alabama 36830
(205) 555-2485

PERMANENT ADDRESS
554 Tremblay Drive
Montgomery, Alabama 36117

OBJECTIVE   To obtain an entry-level position in advertising

EDUCATION

Auburn University, Auburn, Alabama
Expected date of graduation, August, 1992
Degree: Bachelor of Arts
Major: Advertising with a double minor in public relations and marketing

WORK EXPERIENCE

Village Photographers, Auburn, Alabama (Sept. 1991 to present)
Representative to organizations at Auburn University, Auburn University at Montgomery, Lagrange College, Huntingdon College, and Troy State University. Responsibilities include order-handling, customer relations, and preparation of company newsletters.

The Montgomery Advertiser, Montgomery, Alabama (June 1991 to Sept. 1991)
Special studies intern: responsibilities included design and layout of advertisements and ad pages on Harris pagination system, copyediting, and research.

COURSEWORK

Advertising Case Studies, Advertising Campaigns,
Advertising Writing, Market Research, Survey of Research
Methods, Photojournalism, Electronic Field Production,
Marketing for Communication, Broadcast News Writing,
Feature Writing, Newswriting

ACTIVITIES

Sigma Delta Chi journalism honorary, AUPRCA, Advertising Club,
WEGL-91.1 FM news announcer, *Plainsman* (student yearbook) news writer
and copyeditor, Pi Beta Phi national sorority, Alpha Tau Omega Sweetheart,
Auburn Rugby Little Sister

REFERENCES

Mark Warn, Editorial page editor, Montgomery Advertiser (205) 555-1611
Susan Parker, Director, Alabama Christian Day Care (205) 555-1394
Ellen Wilson, Head, Journalism Department, Auburn University (205) 555-8000

PORTFOLIO   Available on request.

Mallory Aiken

7500 N. Washburn
Trenton, New Jersey 08690

201/555-1246 (days)
201/555-0493 (eves)

Career Objective

To gain an entry-level advertising design position where my creative skills in design and illustration can best be utilized.

Education

Bachelor of Fine Arts, May 1992
Southern Illinois University
Carbondale, Illinois
Major: Design
Concentration: Visual Communications
GPA: 4.0 in art; 3.4 overall

Career-Related Skills

• Worked with IBM Publisher's Paintbrush
• Experienced with Macintosh desktop publishing, PageMaker
• Creative and technical drawing skills
• Strong illustration capabilities (pastel, charcoal, air brush)
• Knowledge of Russian and Japanese

Work Experience

Micro Media, Trenton, New Jersey
Reception/Customer Service/Data Entry
Summers 1989 - 1992

Jimmy John's Gourmet Sub Shop, Carbondale, Illinois
Waitress/Sandwich Creator/Cashier
1989 - 1992

Osco Drugs, Trenton, New Jersey
Cashier/Stock Person
1987 - 1989

Kelley Services, Trenton, New Jersey
Office/Clerical Work
1986 - 1988

Interests

Computers, art, photography, music

References

Furnished upon request

Cassidy McLean Brown
2150 Stevens Creek Drive
Salem, Oregon 97310
(503) 555-0928

Objective   A position as Creative Director for a small advertising agency.

Education

- University of Oregon, School of Journalism. Master of Arts Degree, 1985
  Emphasis: Advertising and Public Relations. Wrote graduate thesis on ten-year
  benchmark study of the status of women in newspaper advertising management.

- Oregon State University. Bachelor of Arts, with highest honors, 1979
  Emphasis: English Literature. Wrote honors thesis on Albert Camus' dramatic adaptation of Fyodor
  Dostoevsky's novel, *The Possessed.*

Professional Experience

- Director, ImPrint Services: editing, design, and production for advertisers, 1990-present.

- Instructor, Western Oregon State College, Humanities Division, 1988-90.

- Marketing Director, Jackson Creek Press, 1987-92.

- Associate Editor, *The Oregon Stater* (alumni publication), 1985-87.

- Travel Writer/Correspondent, *Sunset* Magazine, 1984-87.

- Co-Editor and Publisher, CALYX Books, 1985-92. Winner of American Book Award 1990. Currently serving as
  President of the Board.

- Managing Editor for Literature, *CALYX, A Journal of Art and Literature by Women,* 1979-86.

- Communications Director (Acting), Oregon State University Foundation, 1986.

- Marketing Director, Oregon State University Summer Term/Continuing Education, 1986-87.

- Graduate Teaching Fellow, University of Oregon, 1983-85.

Honors

- National Gold Medal Award, Best Feature Article, Council for the Advancement and Support of Education,
  1988, for an article published in *The Oregon Stater,* "The Graying of America"

- National Ace Superior (First Place) Award in the direct mail publications class of the 1988 Agricultural
  Communicators in Education Awards Program

- Research Grant, Gannett Foundation, New York, 1984-85

- Research Grant, Center for the Study of Women in Society, University of Oregon, 1984-85

- Best Thesis Award, University of Oregon, School of Journalism, 1985

- American Business Women's Association Scholarship, 1984

- Graduate Teaching Fellowship, University of Oregon, 1983-85

- Zimmerman Scholarship, University of Oregon, 1983-84

References available on request

FRIEDA M. CARTER

335 West Fifth Street ❖ Brooklyn, NY 12009 ❖ 718/555-8375

❖ ACADEMIC BACKGROUND

Brigham Young University	1988 - 1992
Provo, Utah	
B.A. Communications	April 28, 1992
Minor: Advertising	G.P.A. 3.45
Marshall High School	1984 - 1988
Brooklyn, NY	G.P.A. 3.75

❖ SKILLS AND ACCOMPLISHMENTS

Experienced with purchasing ad space in newspapers and magazines.

Developed concepts for advertising campaign.

Profitably switched ads from publications that produced marginal results to others that produced significantly more productive ones.

Directed and implemented readership survey.

Incorporated analysis from readership survey into market study for presentation to potential advertisers.

Experienced with advertising sales, billing, ad rates, and customer relations.

❖ WORK EXPERIENCE

The Daily Universe	January 1990 - April 1992
Brigham Young University	
Student Newspaper, Provo, Utah	
Advertising Manager	August 1991 - April 1992
Advertising Sales	January 1990 - April 1991
Brooklyn Savings Bank	Summer 1991
Brooklyn, NY	
Advertising Intern	
Rocky Mountain Drive-In	May 1988 - November 1989
Provo, Utah	
Shift Manager, Cook, Counter Waitress	
A&W Restaurant	January 1987 - August 1988
Brooklyn, NY	
Cook, Shift Manager	

❖ REFERENCES   Available on request

Morgan S. Thompson-West

Experience

1986 to present Colby, Stevens, & Hodges New York	Creative Consultant Primary responsibility centers on the dissemination of information about the Scitex 350 Response Electronic Imaging System and the Lightspeed Electronic Design Studio. Other responsibilities include creating and implementing advertising, direct mail, promotions, and events. Serve as a color separation account representative, working with some of the largest advertising agencies and corporations in the New York area.
1971 - 1985 Walsh and Cunningham New York	Vice President/Executive Art Director Responsible for Smooth cigarettes, one of the Top 10 Print Campaigns, according to New York-based Video Storyboard Text (VST) 1982. Other accounts included: WBTM-TV, Tempo cigarettes, Rohrer Packing Company, Miller Company, Jamestown Paper Company, Masonite Corporation, Market Foods, Old Stetsun Beer, Migrator Golf Products, Elan Fishing Equipment, Joy Cosmetics, Marmoset Corporation, and various confidential new products for these and other clients.
1968 - 1971 Marks, Strauss, and Gilbert Chicago	Executive Art Director/Producer Accounts worked on: BankAmericard, M. Jacobs & Sons Clothiers, Central Park Summerfest, Dole Refrigeration, International Garment Workers Guild, Century 21 Realty Corporation, City Center Business Institute, and JFK International Airport.
1966 - 1968 Motorola Corporation Chicago	Corporate Art Director Initiated all advertising and sales promotion materials. Responsible for all art and design purchases. Divisions within corporation worked on: Motorola Cellular Phones, Televisions, Compact Disc and Video Players, Motorola Securities, PGA Golf, Buster Toys, Marx Air Rifles.
1963 - 1966 First National Bank San Francisco	Staff Artist and Advertising Assistant Developed advertising and promotion media packages and camera-ready art.
Additional Data	University of Chicago and University of Illinois. Majored in Graphic Design and Illustration. BFA, 1962 (U. Illinois) Awards: 5 Addy Merit Awards (1982-1984); 62nd Art Directors Club Merit Award (1988); 11 Black Advertising Awards (CEBA) (1982-1986); Certificate of Excellence, Mead Library of Ideas (1978)

References upon request

2820 W. 57th Street • New York, New York 10019 • (212) 555-6685

C A R O L Y N   B.   M A R T E L L I

2210 NW MARINER PLACE ◆ CORAL GABLES, FL 33134 ◆ (305) 555-3321

OBJECTIVE

As a committed career person, I am seeking a challenging, responsible position in the field of advertising design that will utilize my knowledge, skills, and abilities in graphic design while providing opportunities for growth.

EDUCATION

1985 - 1990: California College of Arts and Crafts (CalArts). Bachelor of Fine Arts Degree in Graphic Design. Specialty instruction in computer graphics, advertising design, trademark and logo design.

1983 - 1985: Coral Gables Community College. Studied computer programming and art.

SKILLS

Design and produce thumbnails, roughs, and tight comprehensives to present to clients.

Produce amberlith overlays and amberlith photo-knockout masks.

Layout and paste-up.

Computer graphics using Adobe Illustrator, Aldus Freehand, and VideoMaker on Macintosh IIfx.

Select appropriate type styles and specify type for typesetting.

Obtain bids from printers, color separators, and other service bureaus.

Operate Agfa photostat camera.

Computerized page layout with PageMaker on Macintosh.

Create illustrations in colored pencil, watercolor, graphite, pen and ink, acrylic, and oils.

EXPERIENCE

Worked as free-lance graphic designer for a variety of corporate and individual clients. Involved with design of logos, trademarks, business cards, letterhead, brochures, packaging, and illustration.

Prepared book design, layout, paste-up and production of 148-page book on Macintosh, including four-color cover design.

Completed six pen-and-ink illustrations of homes for Historic Preservation Society of Coral Gables.

Prepared sketches for interior decorator client.

Coordinated a Women's Creative Circle organization.

Worked summers as free-lance interior decor manufacturer.

EXHIBITS

CalArts Student Exhibits, 1986 & 1988 (Award-winners only)
Professor-selected exhibits, 1987, 1988
DesignArts Annual, CalArts Design Student Shows, 1989, 1990
BFA Senior Show, 1990

REFERENCES & PORTFOLIO AVAILABLE

Meghan Scampi
298 South Allston
Cambridge, Massachusetts 02138
(617) 555-5612

Objective
Advertising Sales Director

Symanec Corporation
Cambridge, Massachusetts
December 1986 - present

Senior Sales Support Analyst
Coordinated all aspects of high-level corporate visits for prospective clients requiring participation by management and engineering. Delivered product presentations and demonstrations. Served as Project Manager for a two-year government contract bid.

Field Marketing Specialist
Designed and wrote product marketing guides, competitive reports, and training materials for field representatives. Also responsible for the curriculum and delivery of quarterly System Analyst new hire training classes. The five-day course covered product features, technical information, demonstrations, sales presentations, and workshops.

System Analyst
Responsible for software installation, applications support, troubleshooting, and maintenance of 25 accounts. Symanec Technical Publishing Software runs on Apollo, Digital, Hewlett-Packard, IBM, Macintosh, and Sun hardware.

Mexet Corporation
Boston Headquarters and
Chicago Regional Office
June 1984 - December 1986

Customer Support Manager
Supervised a four-member department that provided telephone support for customer inquiries regarding applications, Unix operating system, and peripherals. Evaluated and assigned priority to account issues, maintained customer records, and compiled weekly statistical reports.

Support Analyst
Presented sales demonstrations for the LiveImage System. Provided training and customer service for installed accounts and assisted in sales office activities.

Compugraphic Corporation
Chicago Regional Office
and St. Louis District Office
June 1982 - June 1984

Classroom Instructor
Promoted to instructor for basic and advanced training courses offered on a classroom basis in the Chicago Regional Office.

Educational Services Representative
Provided on-site applications training for the Modular Composition System, which required extensive national travel. Created a forty-page training supplement adopted for District circulation. Active contributor to *On-Line,* a newsletter for field representatives.

EDUCATION

BS Degree, Art Education, 1979
Radcliffe College, Cambridge, Massachusetts

**CONTINUING
EDUCATION**

Madison Area Technical College, 1980
Commercial art courses in typography, graphic design, and advertising layout

REFERENCES AVAILABLE

St. Louis Community College, 1981 - 1983
Courses in accounting, business administration, data processing, and marketing

A D R I A N   T E R R A K O P F

WORK

HOPES

Advertising
Graphic Design
Copywriting
Graphic Production

DEVICES

Apple Macintosh
Digital VT-220 typesetting terminal
Compugraphic MDT-350 typesetting terminal
Compugraphic 7200-1 headliner
Compugraphic MCS-8400/HS typesetter
Compugraphic Trendsetter 812 typesetter
Chemco Powermatic R650 type processor
Nuarc SST-1418 stat camera
Nuarc VIC-1418 stat camera
Nuarc Rocket 2024 stat camera
Agfa-Gevaert Repromaster 2001 stat camera
Kenro 187 stat camera
Nuarc vacuum frame
Bychrome vacuum easel
Nuarc Astro-Mercury platemaker

SCHOOL

ALSO

Strong command of language and writing. Published several articles in a variety of music-industry magazines and design publications. Wrote reviews for local newspapers. Currently writing a book on the underground music industry.

RESUME

89-92: Jackson Tribune
Page production department; setting and processing type; monitoring typesetting system and wire services; proofreading and page paste-up from editors' dummies (including cropping and scribing photos); placing ads, copy, and headlines; and cutting color overlays.
88-92: Free-lance
Design, illustration, and production work for Summit Information Systems, the Jackson Tribune advertising department, the Cannery Mall, Travel Horizons, The Clothes Tree, Mississippi Commission for the Humanities, and others.
86-88: Sound Around Records
Store manager in 12-unit chain. Supervised advertising, produced and oversaw in-store displays and graphics, and coordinated special events promotions. Handled personnel, inventory, and bookkeeping. Also designed the company logo.
85-85: Everybody's Records
Assistant manager in the same chain that owned Sound Around Records.
83-85: Reilly's Corner Tavern
Bartender, human relations.
83-84: Free-lance
Designed illustrations for record covers for Earth Sound Records. Designed and produced promotional items.
79-83: Happy Trails Used Records
Half-owner. Handled all facets of small-business management, including advertising design, production, and placement in various local media. Designed store logo.

87-89: Jackson Area Community College
A.S. in Graphic Communications. Studied all aspects of graphic design, including basic design, typographic design, corporate identification development, three-dimensional packaging, drawing, illustration, copywriting, desktop publishing, drafting, black and white photography, screenprinting, typesetting, process camera, layout and paste-up, negative imposition, and platemaking.

71-75: Oxford University, Miami, Ohio
Four years in Electrical Engineering, narrowly avoiding a degree.

Present address:
22847 Shore View Road
Jackson, Mississippi 73127
(609) 555-9023
Permanent address:
P.O. Box 22
Jackson, Mississippi 73120
References:
Furnished upon request

Porter Harland
2442 Gallant Road
Charlotte, North Carolina 28215
(704) 555-2856

Objective

Seeking a position as media buyer for a local advertising agency.

Education

Hamline University, St Paul, Minnesota
Bachelor of Science, Journalism/Advertising
Degree Awarded 1990

Experience Summary

— Directed national advertising print media campaign.

— Two years of progressively more responsible experience in media buying and development of media relations.

— Ability to handle every aspect of advertising development, from concept to copywriting to design and production.

— Computer fluent with IBM and Macintosh systems for word processing, graphic design, and page composition utilities.

— Developed and implemented consumer surveys at point-of-purchase outlets.

— Assisted research department with compilation and analysis of survey results.

— Assisted head media buyer with determining strategic plans and media placement alterations based on survey results.

— Maintained records of ad response rates for purposes of evaluation and planning.

Work History

Assistant Media Buyer, Faver-Williams, Inc., Charlotte, NC.
1990 - 1992

Advertising Intern, Marshall Fields, Minneapolis, MN.
Summer and Fall, 1989

Research Assistant, Journalism Department, Hamline University,
St. Paul, MN.
1988 - 1989

Honors

Stevenson Award for Scholarship, 1989

Hamline Foundation Presidential Scholarship, 1988

Dean's Honor Report

Journalism Media Club President, 1989 - 1990

References

Furnished on request

MAE SUJIKAWA ◆ 185 Front Street, N.W. ◆ El Dorado, Kansas 67042 ◆ 316/555-2988

OBJECTIVE Seeking a position as Advertising Manager for a daily newspaper.

CAREER EXPERIENCE

◆ Handle fifteen regular advertising accounts for weekly newspaper.
◆ Charged with developing client base.
◆ Developed sales strategies that posted net increases of 8% over the last quarter.
◆ Increased regular advertiser inches by 12% over one-year period.
◆ Work with design department to develop finished advertisements.
◆ Assist clients with concept development.
◆ Supervise staff of four sales representatives and support staff of two designers, two production artists, and three clerical workers.
◆ Work with Advertising Manager to determine sales projections and budgeting.
◆ Handled twelve major accounts for statewide daily newspaper.
◆ Maintained advertising sales records for entire sales group.
◆ Developed in-house advertisements to promote display ads to potential clients.
◆ Made sales presentations.
◆ Developed and implemented reader survey and prepared analysis for use in demographic fact sheet to send to current and potential advertisers.
◆ Received Top Salesperson of the Month award for three consecutive months.
◆ Responsible for the direction and management of a 25-school district's public information and community relations program.
◆ Assigned and wrote articles on activities, events, and programs pertaining to education.
◆ Prepared all district publications to camera ready status in preparation for printing.

WORK HISTORY

El Dorado Weekly, El Dorado, KS **Advertising Sales Supervisor**	9/90 to present
The Kansas Senior Times, El Dorado, KS **Advertising Sales Representative**	9/89 to 8/90
El Dorado School District, El Dorado, KS **Director of Information**	2/78 to 8/89

EDUCATION

University of Texas, Denton, TX Bachelor of Arts, Liberal Arts	1968 to 1972

REFERENCES   Available on request

Chapter Six

SAMPLE COVER LETTERS

FRIEDA M. CARTER
335 West Fifth Street ❖ Brooklyn, NY 12009 ❖ 718/555-8375

June 30, 1992

Ms. Linda Donaldson
Personnel Director
Brooklyn Savings Bank
12 South Main Street
Brooklyn, NY 12008

Dear Ms. Donaldson:

I am a recent graduate of Brigham Young University and am interested in working for the advertising department at Brooklyn Savings Bank. Ms. Abrams, the advertising director, told me to submit my resume to you for formal application.

As Ms. Abrams will tell you, I spent one summer working for the bank's advertising department as a student intern. I found the work challenging, exciting, and an ideal match for both my academic background and professional interests.

I would like to speak with you at your convenience to discuss employment opportunities and my qualifications. I am available at the number above most mornings before 11:00. Thank you very much for your time.

Sincerely,

Frieda M. Carter

JAMILLA STEWART-LAWRENCE
125 W. Hollis Avenue, No. 6
Charlotte, NC 28230
(704) 555-2789

April 2, 1992

Susan St. James
Personnel Manager
IBM Corporation
22 West Corporate Parkway
Charlotte, NC 28238

Dear Ms. St. James:

In response to the notice posted at the UNC Career Center, I am writing to apply for the promotion/advertising position in your marketing department. After two years of experience in advertising and public relations, I know I can make a significant contribution to your company.

Most recently, I worked as an advertising coordinator in Fort Worth. I'm skilled in copywriting, ad design and layout. One of my responsibilities was creating and publishing the company newsletter; consequently, I have become extremely familiar with Word Perfect word processing and both Aldus PageMaker and Ready, Set, Go desktop publishing applications. Additionally, I was responsible for developing advertising and promotional ideas for new products and grand openings.

As you'll notice from my resume, I also have experience writing for both television and radio. I would like to put my varied background and skills to use in your company, and look forward to your campus visit next month, when I would welcome the opportunity to show you my portfolio. I hope to talk with you soon.

Sincerely,

Jamilla Stewart-Lawrence

554 20th Street, Apt. 22
Philadelphia, PA 19104
March 30, 1992

Ms. Maryann Fuller
Ketchum Communications
Six PPG Plaza
Pittsburgh, PA 15222

Dear Ms. Fuller:

I am writing to inquire about the advertising sales opening at Ketchum Communications. I spoke with your advertising manager, Mr. Fred Hughes, who suggested I send my resume to you in application for the position.

I will graduate from the University of Pennsylvania in June with a Bachelor of Arts in Communications, and I am eager to begin my career in the advertising field.

I completed an internship last year in the public relations department of A. Martin, Inc. My responsibilities there included assisting the staff in market and product research, demographics and psychographics, and advertising concept and strategy planning. This practical experience, combined with an education that honed my copywriting and communication skills, provides qualifications that will be a plus for your organization.

Thank you for reviewing the enclosed resume. I will contact you next week in order to arrange a future meeting at your convenience.

Sincerely,

Karl P. Welch

Richard L. Chin
4365 Woodruff Ave #45
Lakewood, CA 90713

February 25, 1992

Mr. Paul Gill
ARL Publishing Group
Los Angeles, CA 90032

Dear Mr. Gill,

I am responding to your ad in Sunday's paper regarding the Advertising Production Coordinator position. I have been working in the graphic design field for the past three years and have completed a wide range of projects involving ad creation, development, and design.

I feel my creative style, my computer expertise, and my dedication to being the best that I can be make me a viable candidate for your position. My specific experience as the production coordinator for a printing firm gives me far more than the basic requirements listed in your advertisement.

Enclosed please find my resume. I hope we can arrange a time for an interview to explore potential opportunities. Thank you for your consideration.

Sincerely,

Richard L. Chin

879 Hawthorne Street
Melrose Park, IL 60164

April 13, 1992

Larsen Communications
2315 North Valley
Chester, IL 60646

Dear Sir or Madam:

I am writing in response to your ad in the Sunday Tribune, and am enclosing a resume, which outlines my previous employment and education relevant to the advertising design position with Larsen Communications.

I have acquired many valuable skills from my work experience and education in the communications and design fields. I have used PageMaker and Quark XPress, paired with design logic and sketching skills, to develop designs for products, as well as advertising and promotion materials for those products. As PR Manager at Talbott, Inc., I was responsible for all public relations and promotion, which included supervising all advertising accounts.

I would like an opportunity to discuss my qualifications and interest in your organization, and can be reached at 708.555-1221. I appreciate your time and consideration, and look forward to hearing from you.

Sincerely,

Kristine Rabinski

259 W North Avenue
Baltimore, MD 21202
18 April 1992

Vera Hampton
Advertising Director
Publicity Specialists, Inc.
7432 Orleans Street
Baltimore, MD 21231

Dear Ms. Hampton:

I am writing to inquire about current position openings involving graphics and advertising with your firm. I noticed your general employment announcement in the Career Center at Maryland University, where I am currently a graduating senior.

The enclosed resume outlines my managerial experience, as well as my strong background in ~~product~~ advertising, both in developing advertising campaigns and in design. Prior to returning to Maryland University, I worked for twelve years as a designer and account manager for a small design firm which specialized in advertising.

I am interested in a meeting to discuss my capabilities, and will call you next week to inquire about setting up an interview. Thank you for your consideration.

Sincerely,

Marcus J. Reed

225 Delgado Street
Santa Fe, NM 87501
25 April 1992

Ms. Barbara Savoy
Allegre Advertising Agency
3990 Paseo del Sol
Santa Fe, NM 87501

Dear Ms Savoy:

I am writing at the suggestion of Marilyn Sander, the head of graphic design in your agency. She mentioned the possibility of current openings in account management.

I have recently relocated to Santa Fe and am looking for work in the advertising and promotion fields. My skills and interests lie in the development and coordination of advertising campaigns. While managing the advertising department of New England Alliance, I developed concepts, designed ads, supervised layout and typesetting, and coordinated all media placement.

My training in communication and design is extensive, and my experience has prepared me for successfully supervising both projects and the people who must work together to make a campaign happen.

Please review the enclosed resume. I would like to meet with you at your convenience. Thank you for your time and consideration.

Yours truly,

Gloria Santos

583 Rampart Avenue
Akron, OH 44313

30 March 1992

L. Conner
Capitol Communications
359 Main Street
Akron, OH 44308

Dear L. Conner:

I write in reference to your advertisement for an Advertising Director, which appeared in the March 28 edition of the *News-Time*. I believe my background and experience are well-matched to your needs.

My broad education and work record evolved from employment with ad agencies, design studios, publishing companies, newspapers, corporate art departments, and a TV station. As a freelance graphic artist/desktop publisher, I have acquired experience with a wide variety of organizations. I have created and produced advertisements and have also developed and implemented national advertising and publicity campaigns.

I would like to discuss the position further, and will telephone you early next week to set up a possible meeting at your convenience. Thank you for your consideration.

Sincerely,

Janis L. Gould

Judith A. Washington

958 NW Sycamore, Amarillo, Texas 78077   806/555-0944

28 November 1992

Thomas V. Walker
President
Dallas Dimensions, Inc.
14 East Patterson
Dallas, Texas 75221

Dear Mr. Walker:

I was delighted to receive notification of the availability of the Production Manager's position at Dallas Dimensions. Having visited your offices on several occasions, I have been tremendously impressed with your facilities and the organization's professionalism.

In reply to your kind note, I would like to submit the enclosed resume and letters of recommendation for your consideration. The variety of projects I've handled and the range of clients I've served during my years as a freelancer will, I believe, place me in an advantageous position to contribute significantly to your company's future growth.

I look forward to having an opportunity to talk with you further about the position, the challenges it will provide and the expertise with which I am prepared to meet those challenges. I will telephone you early next week to set up a time at your convenience. Thank you again for letting me know about the opening.

Best regards,

Judith A. Washington

Richard Walker

2774 Tower Drive • Chicago, Illinois 60647 • (708) 555-8831

September 24, 1992

T. Barker
Jameson Publishing Group
2261 S. Queen Street
Chicago, IL 60635

Dear T. Barker:

I am writing in response to your recent advertisement in the *Chicago Tribune* for an advertising production/promotion coordinator. I am very interested in the position, for this appeals to be the challenge and opportunity I seek in the field of production design.

In addition, I believe I'm right for the job. The enclosed resume provides the details, but the following professional highlights from my record are in keeping with your position requirements:

Should Reflect my experience.

- 15 years as a graphic artist and designer
- 12 years experience in advertising design and production
- Expert with desktop publishing software and hardware
- 8 years management and supervisory experience

In addition to an extensive professional background, I have kept current with the vast changes being made in electronic design, publishing, and pre-press, and can confidently say that I am at the high end of the learning curve the entire industry is currently experiencing.

Thank you for your consideration, and I look forward to having an opportunity to share with you a portfolio of some of my work.

Sincerely yours,

Richard Walker

IAN P. ROBINSON
1009 Selby Drive, Geneva, Illinois 60134
708/555-9984

August 26, 1992

Director
Benchley, Faber & Associates, Inc.
P.O. Box 2568-D
Chicago, IL 60629

To the Director:

Please accept the enclosed resume in application for the Advertising Account Manager position announced in the August 20 issue of the *Chicago Times*.

Perhaps the most important benefit I can offer Benchley, Faber & Associates is my extensive experience as a buyer of the kind of advertising services you offer. By bringing the perspective of the "account" into the position of account manager, I believe I can contribute significantly to positive client-agency relations.

In addition, my background in design and production enabled me to augment sales at my most recent post by some 35% during my four-year tenure. I developed, produced and implemented direct mail and newspaper advertising campaigns for an exclusive French import company.

I would like to arrange an opportunity to talk with you further about the position and my qualifications. I may be reached at (708) 555-0228 weekdays and the number above evenings and weekends. I look forward to hearing from you.

Sincerely,

Ian P. Robinson

Timony Blaisdell
P.O. Box 216B3
Boise, Idaho 83702

12 October 1992

Director
Rocky Mountain Magazine
P.O. Box RM
Denver, Colorado 80201

Dear Sir/Madam:

In response to your recent advertisement in *AdWeek,* I would like to submit my professional resume for the position of Advertising Director.

My current role as Advertising Director of the daily newspaper, *The Boise Sun,* has provided tremendous challenges over the past seven years, but I am interested in exploring new growth opportunities, and magazine advertising is the natural next step. I have also held positions in marketing and promotion, and those skills appear to be high on your list of qualifications for the position.

Although currently living in Boise, I am quite happy to travel to Denver to talk with you at your convenience. I will call you early next week to inquire about your schedule. Thank you for considering the enclosed resume.

Yours sincerely,

Timony Blaisdell

1590 Junction Boulevard
Lexington, KY 40506

May 15, 1992

Advertising Manager
Dodd Brothers Advertising
44 West Benchley
Lexington, KY 40509

Dear Sir or Madam:

I recently received notification through the University of Kentucky School of Journalism that you are looking for qualified advertising copywriters. Please accept the enclosed resume in application for one of these positions.

As a graduate of the graduate journalism program at the UK, I have received extensive training in the field of advertising, including the opportunity to serve as the Advertising Coordinator for the university's public relations office. In this capacity, I have been responsible for directing and developing all advertisements and promotional materials, including radio and television commercials, newspaper and magazine display ads, brochures, posters, and flyers. I have written the copy for everything that came out of the office since January of 1990.

I would appreciate an opportunity to share some examples of the past two years' productivity. I believe you will find my background and experience fully qualify me for the position of advertising copywriter. I look forward to talking with you.

Sincerely,

Cheryl Scott

23 Battersea Street
Portland, ME 04129

26 July 1992

Corporate Director
Box 246C
c/o *Maine Herald*
845 Jefferson Avenue
Portland, ME 04129

To the Agency Director:

In reply to the advertisement posted in the July 18 edition of the *Maine Herald,* I would like to apply for the position of advertising director.

My interest in your advertisement was piqued by the description of your company as involved with primary products manufacturing. I have 15 years experience as an advertising specialist, working primarily with timber, agriculture, and steel producers. My background includes work with both broadcast and print media, and I have won national awards for both advertising concepts and the results achieved by two different advertising campaigns.

I would like to have an opportunity to learn more about your organization and how my expertise can make a positive contribution to your advertising efforts. Please telephone me at your convenience. I am available at (207) 555-9365 most mornings. Thank you for your time and attention.

Sincerely,

Edward G. McDonald

Gary A. Azukas
2245 Haven Street
Rumford, Maine 04276
(207) 555-9197 (D)
(207) 555-2983 (E)

John Garcia
Advertising Director
WMTV
5 Broadcast Lane
Portland, ME 04277

Dear Mr. Garcia:

I am writing to inquire about the position of assistant advertising director listed in the March edition of Broadcast News. If the position is still vacant, I would very much like to apply. My professional resume is enclosed.

As my resume indicates, I have had five years of experience with video production and editing for an organization that develops television commercials and documentaries for a wide range of clients. I have also been on the buying end of television advertising, as well as involved with developing market information with which to make strategic plans for television advertising campaigns.

After giving you an opportunity to review the enclosed resume, I will give you a call late next week to see about setting up a time when we can talk further about both the position and my qualifications. Thank you very much for your consideration.

Sincerely,

Gary A. Azukas

33 West Arthur Place
Boca Raton, Florida 33486

November 18, 1992

Advertising Sales Manager
Boca Raton News
P.O. Box 1219
Boca Raton, FL 33481

Dear Sir or Madam:

I will be graduating from the Florida Atlantic College
School of Journalism next month, and I would like to
apply for a position in advertising sales with the Boca
Raton News.

I am currently working part-time at the Advertiser, but
would very much like to seek full-time work with
opportunity to expand my sphere of activity to include
display advertising as well as classifieds. My experience
as the advertising manager of the student newspaper at
FAC has given me the skills and salesmanship I believe
you are looking for.

My term will end November 29, and I will call you early
in the following week to see if there might be a
convenient time for us to meet and discuss the position
further. If you would like to reach me in the meantime, I
am available most afternoons at 555-2756. Thank you for
your consideration in reviewing the enclosed resume.

Sincerely,

Christina Benson

Morgan S. Thompson-West

October 4, 1992

Ruth McLennan
United Airlines
Corporate Advertising Division
1100 Madison Avenue, 20th Floor
New York, NY 10015

Dear Ms. McLennan

In response to your recent advertisement in the New York Times for a print advertising art director, I am enclosing a brief resume and some samples of the well-known trademarks that I have been responsible for in previous employment.

During the past four years I have handled corporate identity, product development, advertising, and collateral for such clients as JFK International Airport, WBTM-TV, Brooklyn Medical Association, and Eastside Event Center. I have also provided creative services to New York National Savings Bank, Raymond Insurance Agents, and agencies such as Lyle Barnett, P. Richard Thompson, and Tracy & Associates.

My strengths lie in creativity, print production, and management—essential skills for the advertising art director for a major corporation. I hope we can arrange an interview at your convenience to discuss what challenges the position offers and the skills and experience I can bring to your organization.

With best regards,

Morgan S. Thompson-West

2820 W. 57th Street • New York, New York 10019 • (212) 555-6685

15829 First Avenue
Battle Creek, MI 49017

February 12, 1992

Carolyn Wheatley
Personnel Director
Denby & Associates, Inc.
Advertising Management Specialists
4317 Market Street, Suite 117
Chicago, IL 60619

Dear Ms. Wheatley:

I am responding to your recent advertisement for an assistant traffic manager position with your organization. Enclosed with this letter of introduction is my resume, which will give you an overview of my education and experiences. I am sure you will find my background suited to your needs.

I hold two Associates degrees in graphic design and printing. This diversified education prepared me for my employment with several printing organizations, leading to my current role as Production Manager of the Battle Creek Reporter, Michigan's second-largest newspaper. As production manager, I am involved in many facets of the publishing process and have gained extensive experience in employee supervision and public relations.

I look forward to the opportunity to meet with you to discuss my qualifications further. I will call your office next week to arrange a possible meeting. Thank you for your time and consideration.

Sincerely,

James Marchington
(616) 555-9042

MARY E. GLANCY
72 College Street
Beloit, Wisconsin 53511
(608) 555-4267

March 17, 1992

Mr. Albert Quentin, Manager
Advertising Department
The Beloit Monthly
Second Avenue & Market Street
Beloit, Wisconsin 53511

Dear Mr. Quentin:

As a recent graduate of Beloit College, I am preparing to pursue a career in advertising and publishing. I would like to apply for the advertising copywriter's position announced in the Sunday *Times*.

At Beloit, I served as Advertising Coordinator for the college newspaper, which consisted of a readership of approximately 4,000. I was responsible for ad sales and ad production. Because it was such a small paper, I was often involved in many aspects of publishing, including news writing, layout, advertising design, and production. This experience, along with my strong eye for detail, an ability to read quickly and efficiently, and my computer proficiency would prove valuable to your organization.

I am enclosing a resume with more specific descriptions of my qualifications. I will furnish references upon request. Thank you for your time and consideration.

Sincerely,

Mary E. Glancy

3335 North Road
Bellevue, Colorado 80512
303 555-4886

June 15, 1992

Director of Advertising Sales
Finley Stern, Inc.
32 Boulder Avenue
Denver, Colorado 80236

Dear Director:

I am writing to you because I believe my education, work experience and interests would make me an asset to your advertising sales department. If you anticipate any job openings in the near future, please consider my resume in application for a position in advertising sales.

I recently graduated from Colorado State University with a bachelor's degree in Journalism. My major coursework in advertising and design, advertising copywriting, and publication management was supplemented with business courses in marketing, sales, and planning.

Beyond my education, I have practical experience. To put myself through college I took a clerical job at a local magazine in December 1985. Seven months later I became the magazine's advertising sales representative and held that position for another two years. Because the magazine was a small one, I also worked on all aspects of the publication, from writing and editing to design, production, and circulation. It was here that I first began to test the skills I was learning in college.

This experience helped me to win an internship last summer, during which I worked as an advertising account assistant for a company that represents over 25 national corporations. I assumed immediate responsibility for two regional corporate accounts.

If you feel there may be a place for me at Finley Stern, I would be delighted to further discuss how my qualifications might be of value to you. I look forward to hearing from you.

Yours truly,

Jolene E. Marks

VGM CAREER BOOKS

OPPORTUNITIES IN
Available in both paperback and hardbound editions

Accounting
Acting
Advertising
Aerospace
Agriculture
Airline
Animal and Pet Care
Architecture
Automotive Service
Banking
Beauty Culture
Biological Sciences
Biotechnology
Book Publishing
Broadcasting
Building Construction Trades
Business Communication
Business Management
Cable Television
Carpentry
Chemical Engineering
Chemistry
Child Care
Chiropractic Health Care
Civil Engineering
Cleaning Service
Commercial Art and Graphic Design
Computer Aided Design and
  Computer Aided Mfg.
Computer Maintenance
Computer Science
Counseling & Development
Crafts
Culinary
Customer Service
Dance
Data Processing
Dental Care
Direct Marketing
Drafting
Electrical Trades
Electronic and Electrical Engineering
Electronics
Energy
Engineering
Engineering Technology
Environmental
Eye Care
Fashion
Fast Food
Federal Government
Film
Financial
Fire Protection Services
Fitness
Food Services
Foreign Language
Forestry
Gerontology
Government Service
Graphic Communications
Health and Medical
High Tech
Home Economics
Hospital Administration
Hotel & Motel Management
Human Resources Management
  Careers
Information Systems
Insurance
Interior Design
International Business
Journalism
Laser Technology
Law

Law Enforcement and Criminal Justice
Library and Information Science
Machine Trades
Magazine Publishing
Management
Marine & Maritime
Marketing
Materials Science
Mechanical Engineering
Medical Technology
Metalworking
Microelectronics
Military
Modeling
Music
Newspaper Publishing
Nursing
Nutrition
Occupational Therapy
Office Occupations
Opticiany
Optometry
Packaging Science
Paralegal Careers
Paramedical Careers
Part-time & Summer Jobs
Performing Arts
Petroleum
Pharmacy
Photography
Physical Therapy
Physician
Plastics
Plumbing & Pipe Fitting
Podiatric Medicine
Postal Service
Printing
Property Management
Psychiatry
Psychology
Public Health
Public Relations
Purchasing
Real Estate
Recreation and Leisure
Refrigeration and Air Conditioning
Religious Service
Restaurant
Retailing
Robotics
Sales
Sales & Marketing
Secretarial
Securities
Social Science
Social Work
Speech-Language Pathology
Sports & Athletics
Sports Medicine
State and Local Government
Teaching
Technical Communications
Telecommunications
Television and Video
Theatrical Design & Production
Transportation
Travel
Trucking
Veterinary Medicine
Visual Arts
Vocational and Technical
Warehousing
Waste Management
Welding
Word Processing
Writing
Your Own Service Business

CAREERS IN
Accounting; Advertising; Business; Communications; Computers; Education; Engineering; Health Care; High Tech; Law; Marketing; Medicine; Science

CAREER DIRECTORIES
Careers Encyclopedia
Dictionary of Occupational Titles
Occupational Outlook Handbook

CAREER PLANNING
Admissions Guide to Selective
  Business Schools
Career Planning and Development for
  College Students and Recent
  Graduates
Careers Checklists
Careers for Animal Lovers
Careers for Bookworms
Careers for Culture Lovers
Careers for Foreign Language
  Aficionados
Careers for Good Samaritans
Careers for Gourmets
Careers for Nature Lovers
Careers for Numbers Crunchers
Careers for Sports Nuts
Careers for Travel Buffs
Guide to Basic Resume Writing
Handbook of Business and
  Management Careers
Handbook of Health Care Careers
Handbook of Scientific and
  Technical Careers
How to Change Your Career
How to Choose the Right Career
How to Get and Keep
  Your First Job
How to Get into the Right Law School
How to Get People to Do Things
  Your Way
How to Have a Winning Job Interview
How to Land a Better Job
How to Make the Right Career Moves
How to Market Your College Degree
How to Prepare a *Curriculum Vitae*
How to Prepare for College
How to Run Your Own Home Business
How to Succeed in Collge
How to Succeed in High School
How to Write a Winning Resume
Joyce Lain Kennedy's Career Book
Planning Your Career of Tomorrow
Planning Your College Education
Planning Your Military Career
Planning Your Young Child's
  Education
Resumes for Advertising Careers
Resumes for College Students & Recent
  Graduates
Resumes for Communications Careers
Resumes for Education Careers
Resumes for High School Graduates
Resumes for High Tech Careers
Resumes for Sales and Marketing Careers
Successful Interviewing for College
  Seniors

SURVIVAL GUIDES
Dropping Out or Hanging In
High School Survival Guide
College Survival Guide

VGM Career Horizons
a division of *NTC Publishing Group*
4255 West Touhy Avenue
Lincolnwood, Illinois 60646-1975